WRI GUIDES

STEP-BY-STEP INDIVIDUALIZED INSTRUCTION

MW01710155

Third Edition

Sandra Panman, M.P.S.
State University of New York at New Paltz

Richard Panman, Ph.D.
State University of New York at New Paltz

Active Learning Corporation

New Paltz, New York/(914) 255-0844

Address all inquiries to:

Active Learning Corporation
P.O. Box 254
New Paltz, NY 12561
Phone: (914) 255-0844 Fax: (914) 255-8796

Cover Concept: Michael Parman
Cover Artist: Sergio Diaz

Text Design, Editing and Montage: Linda Gluck

Art Director, Illustrations: Elena Erber
Illustrator: Kirk Van Deusen

Printed in the United States of America/97mv

ISBN: 0-912813-25-3 *3rd Edition*

We dedicate this book to our children, Lisa and Seth, for their love, patience and understanding.

Acknowledgments

For permission to reprint copyrighted material, grateful acknowledgment is made to the following sources:

The Atlantic Monthly Company: Excerpted from "The Scarlet Ibis" by James Hurst. Copyright © 1960, by the Atlantic Monthly Company, Boston, Mass. 02116. Reprinted with permission.

A. S. Barnes & Company, Inc. and Kaye and Ward Limited: From *Modern Spearfishing* by I. S. Ivanovic. Copyright © 1955 by A. S. Barnes & Company, Inc.

Ray Bradbury: Excerpted from "A Sound of Thunder." Copyright © 1952 by Ray Bradbury Enterprises / A California Corporation.

John Henrik Clarke: "The Boy Who Painted Christ Black." Copyright © 1940 by John Henrik Clarke.

Don Congdon Associates, Inc.: "All the Years of Her Life" by Morley Callaghan. Copyright © 1935, renewed 1962 by Morley Callaghan.

Dodd, Mead & Company, Inc.: "The Monkey's Paw," from *Lady of The Barge* by W. W. Jacobs. Copyright © 1902 by Dodd, Mead & Company.

Faber & Faber, Ltd.: Excerpted from *As I Saw the U.S.A.* by Jan Morris. Copyright © 1956.

Random House, Inc.: "Table" and "Working Girl" from *Sentence Combining: A Composing Book* by William Strong. Copyright © 1973 by Random House, Inc.

William Saroyan: "Gaston" and an excerpt from "An Ornery Kind of Kid" by William Saroyan. Permission granted by the Estate of William Saroyan.

We offer our gratitude and thanks to our many friends and colleagues for their suggestions, critical comments and encouragement.

Contents

Introduction

From the time that the first drawing appeared on a cave wall, human beings have had a need to communicate in writing. Early writers used pictures to express feelings and thoughts. Today, the use of written language enables us to express a wide range of emotions and ideas. The ability to write well can be a great asset in school, at work, and in our personal lives. The goal of *Writing Guides* is to help students develop confidence and competence as writers.

I LEARN

This program is based on principles of learning that can be used to teach people almost anything, from riding a bicycle to piloting a space shuttle. The acronym *I LEARN* summarizes the names of these principles: **I**mitation, **L**earning rate, **E**ncouragement, **A**ctive practice, **R**evision, and **N**ew tasks. We have applied these principles to writing instruction because they work so well.

Writing Guides uses models written by well known authors. Students are asked to **imitate** these examples as they create their own compositions. This has proven to be a very effective and efficient way of learning.

One of the things that students like best about this individualized program is that it allows them to work at their own **learning rate**. Setting individual goals eliminates competition with other students and makes learning a pleasant experience.

The text is filled with activities that are realistic and attainable. Being able to successfully complete an activity **encourages** students to achieve further success. Since the teacher spends very little time lecturing in class, she/he can give personal attention and regular feedback to each student.

This program requires the student to **actively practice** reading and writing on a regular basis. As a result, both reading and writing skills show dramatic improvement.

The opportunity to **revise** work without penalty helps students to reduce errors and improve their writing. This is reflected in both better grades and in positive attitudes toward learning.

Learning to write is a developmental process. Each **new task** in the text incorporates learning from previous lessons. The step-by-step nature of this instruction enables the student to experience success on a regular basis which in turn promotes self-confidence.

Organization

Writing Guides consists of forty-eight work units, or guides, which are divided into four major sections: Sentence Skills, The Paragraph, About Fiction, and Letters and Reports. Early units develop skills such as writing complete sentences, using transitional words and phrases, and sentence combining. Later guides help the student to write paragraphs, short stories, reports, persuasive essays, and research papers. Each of the writing guides clearly specifies what is to be learned and how to master the task.

Each guide begins with a model of the type of writing the student is expected to master. The model is followed by prewriting activities which focus on the concepts to be learned. The student then creates an original composition by imitating the model, has his work evaluated, and completes corrective exercises recommended by the instructor. The student writes a second composition of the same type based on selected reading materials made available by the instructor. An answer key for the Practice (prewriting) exercises is included in the text. Prewriting activities are a part of each writing guide.

The Student Management Forms which accompany the book explain how the program works and make record keeping easy for both student and teacher. The management system helps to create a learning environment which minimizes competition while generating new expectations and outcomes. Students do not compete with one another for grades. The assumption is that every student will master the material. Both student and instructor can look forward to a positive working relationship in a relaxed and productive atmosphere.

If you are using this book on your own, outside of a classroom setting, no teacher will be available to evaluate your work. Ask a person whose opinion you respect—friend, colleague, or relative—to read your papers and give you feedback. Ask them to tell you what they learned from your paper, what they liked and disliked about it, and what was clear or unclear about the paper. Make revisions based on their comments and the Checklist in each lesson.

To The Teacher

Feedback from the teacher can have a very powerful and positive effect in motivating the student to learn. Make sure students understand your system for evaluating and grading papers. To gain students' trust and confidence, try to give them the good news first, followed by your constructive criticism. The good news is praise for at least one aspect of the student's paper: ideas, choice of subject, enthusiasm, neat handwriting, etc.

When there are many errors in a paper, focus on three or four of the most frequent ones. As these are eliminated, you can point out others. Try not to overwhelm your students with criticism before they develop confidence in their ability to write. Written comments should be specific enough for the student to make changes and corrections in their work. You may also want to speak with the student in a brief, one-to-one informal conference in class. Conferences allow for discussion and direct exchange of ideas.

Two valuable and enjoyable classroom activities that you can use with the text are brainstorming and peer critiquing. While composition exercises provide suggested topics, you may wish to have students "brainstorm" as a group to generate other topics. From time to time, completed compositions can be critiqued by the members of the class (peer group). Prepare students for this by sharing the feedback guidelines above and encouraging constructive criticism. Brainstorming and peer critiquing give students opportunities to sharpen their listening and speaking skills, as well as improve writing ability.

WRITING GUIDES

I.
Sentence Skills

Basic writing skills are the tools that you will need for all writing activities. Each new skill that you acquire will help to make writing easier and more enjoyable.

The first guide, Writing Appraisal I, will be used to compare your writing abilities at the beginning and end of this course. The other guides teach sentence skills and prepare you for writing paragraphs.

Guides

1.

Writing Appraisal I

It is important that the person evaluating your work can read what you have written. The first part of this guide will help you to practice your handwriting. Even those who write clearly can benefit from this review.

The story below is called an anecdote. **An anecdote is a short, often entertaining description of an incident.** Read the following anecdote.

A MATTER OF TASTE

Two goats in the desert found a tin of film. One of them nuzzled it until the lid came off. The film leader loosened around the spool, and the goat ate a few frames.

The second goat ate some, too. Soon, they pulled all the film off the reel and consumed the whole of it. When nothing was left but the can and the spool, the first goat said,

"Wasn't that great?"

"Oh, I don't know," replied the second goat. "I thought the book was better."

Handwriting Practice

Follow the steps outlined below:

- Copy the anecdote in script.
- Copy those lines from the Handwriting Model (next page) that are marked with an asterisk (*).
- Now, copy the anecdote again.

When you complete this exercise, go on to the Composition part of the guide.

Handwriting Model

Upper Case (Capitals)

* A B C D E F G H I
* J K L M N O P Q R
* S T U V W X Y Z

Lower Case (small letters)

* a b c d e f g h i j k l m
* n o p q r s t u v w x y z

Some small letters are half the size of capital letters.

* a c e i m n o r s u v w x

Some small letters use almost as much space as capital letters.
These are written above and/or below the line.

* b d f g h j k l p q t y z

Letters within words are equally spaced.

spacing spacing spacing

Slant all letters in one direction.

style style style

Composition

This exercise will provide you and your instructor with a sample of your writing at the beginning of this program. When you complete the course, you will write another sample and be able to appraise (measure) how much progress you have made. Write **three** paragraphs according to the instructions given.

Narration Write a paragraph of **five** complete sentences that tells a story about one of the following events:

an embarrassing situation

something that changed my life

the best day of my life

a frightening experience

Description Write a paragraph of **five** complete sentences that describes one of the following subjects:

a face

a bakery

a cut finger

a sunset

Explanation Write a paragraph of **five** complete sentences that explains how to do one of the following:

apply make-up

catch a fish

cook something

help someone who is choking

Submit the completed writing assignment and Handwriting Practice to your instructor for evaluation.

2.

Using the Dictionary

This guide will help you to review use of the dictionary. Here is a sample dictionary entry and a key to its parts.

THE DICTIONARY ENTRY

sur.prise /sə(r)-prīz/ *n* [ME, fr. MF, fr. fem. of surpris]

1. an attack made without warning
2. something that surprises
3. the state of being surprised

Syn. ASTONISHMENT

KEY TO THE DICTIONARY ENTRY

entry word:	sur.prise (two syllables)
pronunciation:	sə(r)-prīz
part of speech:	n (noun)
origin of word:	[ME, fr. MF, fr. fem. of surpris]
numbered definitions:	1, 2, 3
synonym (Syn.):	ASTONISHMENT

Practice

Read each part of the following exercise and answer all **43** questions. Refer to the Dictionary Entry and Key to complete numbers one through six.

1. What entry word is given? ______________________

Write the three definitions given for the entry word.

2. ______________________
3. ______________________
4. ______________________

The Synonym

The last line of the dictionary entry begins with **Syn.** This is an abbreviation for the word synonym. Look this word up in the dictionary. What does this word mean? Write the definition in the space below.

5. synonym: ______________________

6. Write the synonym that the Dictionary Entry gives for the word *surprise.* ______________________

Use the dictionary to find a synonym for the first word in each row of words below. Write the word in each group that is a synonym for the first word.

7.	**unique** —	unusual	ordinary	precise	binding
8.	**cabaret** —	headpiece	vehicle	nightclub	prison
9.	**gnat** —	rat	horse	bird	fly
10.	**serene** —	ceiling	peaceful	spoiled	clean
11.	**snafu** —	confusion	flute	snail	balloon

It is important to know **exactly** where a word fits alphabetically, so you can find it in the dictionary.

Alphabetizing

Listed below are ten words. Arrange these words in alphabetical order, and number them 12 through 21.

hollow	owl	12. ________	17. ________
entrance	sugar	13. ________	18. ________
digest	write	14. ________	19. ________
middle	kitten	15. ________	20. ________
confront	quiet	16. ________	21. ________

Listed below are ten words. All of these words begin with the same letter. Arrange these words in alphabetical order, and number them 22 through 31. Since each word begins with the letter *P*, alphabetize according to the second letter of the word. If that is the same, alphabetize according to the third, etc.

pioneer	predict	22. ________	27. ________
pure	plenty	23. ________	28. ________
pleasant	prepare	24. ________	29. ________
proud	pronounce	25. ________	30. ________
probe	pretty	26. ________	31. ________

grisly ● grouch

gris·ly \'griz-lē\ *adj* **gris·li·er; -est** [ME, fr. OE *grislic,* fr. *gris-* (akin to OE *āgrīsan* to fear); akin to OHG *grīsenlīh* terrible] **1** : inspiring horror or intense fear : FORBIDDING ⟨houses that were dark and ~ under the blank, cold sky —D. H. Lawrence⟩ **2** : inspiring disgust or distaste ⟨a ~ account of the fire⟩ — **gris·li·ness** *n*
²grit *vb* **grit·ted; grit·ting** *vi* : to give forth a grating sound ~ *vt* **1** : to cover or spread with grit; *esp* : to smooth (as marble) by means of a coarse abrasive **2** : to cause (as one's teeth) to grind or grate
¹griz·zle \'griz-əl\ *n* [ME *grisel,* adj., gray, fr. MF, fr. *gris,* of Gmc origin; akin to OHG *grīs* gray] **1** *archaic* : gray hair **2 a** : a roan coat pattern or color **b** : a gray or roan animal
grizzly bear *n* : a very large powerful typically brownish yellow bear (*Ursus horribilis*) of the uplands of western No. America — called also *grizzly*
gro *abbr* gross
groan \'grōn\ *vb* [ME *gronen,* fr. OE *grānian;* akin to OHG *grīnan* to growl] *vi* **1** : to utter a deep moan indicative of pain, grief, or ... **2** : to make a harsh ... creaking) under sud... strain ~ *vt* : to ...
groan·er *n*
¹groat \'gr... *usu pl* ... lar...

grizzly bear

... or ... any of a ...y having pol- ...aic : MAN, FELLOW **2** ... of several officers of the ...or boy in charge of the feed- ...horses **3** : BRIDEGROOM ...re for (as a horse) **2** : to make neat ...ly ~*ed* woman⟩ **3** : to get into readi- ...ctive : PREPARE ⟨was being ~*ed* as a presi- ... ~ *vi* : to groom oneself ...nər\ *n* : one who grooms (as dogs) ...n \'grümz-mən, 'grumz-\ *n* : a male friend who attends ...groom at his wedding
...ove \'grüv\ *n* [ME *groof;* akin to OE *grafan* to dig — more at GRAVE] **1** : a long narrow channel or depression **2 a** : a fixed routine : RUT **b** : a situation suited to one's abilities or interests : NICHE **3** : top form ⟨a great talker when he is in the ~⟩ **4** : the line or course to follow for best results ⟨his every pitch was right in the ~⟩ **5** : an enjoyable, pleasurable, or exciting experience
²groove *vb* **grooved; groov·ing** *vt* **1 a** : to make a groove in **b** : to join by a groove **2 a** : to enjoy appreciatively ⟨~*s* exciting experiences⟩ **b** : ... ⟨*grooving* —Steph... by a groove **2** : ... : experience keen... porary minds an...
groov·er *n*
groovy \'grü-vē\ ... EXCELLENT ⟨f... mention ...
grope ... ak... ...al pr... ...uced in ...
...u·lar \'gräs... ...ame of the goosel...
gros·su·la·rite \-l... colorless or green, ...
grosz \'grósh\ *n,* ... table
grot \'grät\ *n* [MF ...
¹gro·tesque \grō-'... *tesca,* lit., cave pai... : a style of deco... human and anima... figures that may ... caricature **b** : a ... tesque **3** : SANS S...
²grotesque *adj* : ... grotesque: as **a** : ... : departing marke... *syn* see FANTASTIC
gro·tes·que·rie *als...* *tesque* + *-erie* -ery ... ity or state of bein...
grot·to \'grät-(,)ō\ ... L *crypta* cavern, c... ture made to resen...
grouch \'grauch\ ... bad temper **b** : ... nutes —W. A. W... person : GRUMBLE...

Guide Words

Two guide words are printed at the top of each page of the dictionary. The first guide word represents the first entry on a page. The second guide word represents the last entry on that page. All of the words listed on the page are in alphabetical order between the two guide words.

In the following exercise, the guide word *grisly* represents the first entry on a dictionary page. The second guide word, *grouch,* is the last entry on that page.

There are twelve entry words listed below. Some of these are on the same page in the dictionary as the guide words, *grisly* and *grouch.* The remaining entry words are on the other pages in the dictionary. Use the guide words to help you complete the exercise below.

- Write the letter *s* for those entries that belong on the same page as the guide words.
- Write the letter *b* for those entries that come before this page.
- Write the letter *a* for those words that come after this page.

Entry Words		
	32. ________ guard	38. ________ growl
	33. ________ groom	39. ________ griddle
	34. ________ grill	40. ________ guarantee
	35. ________ grieve	41. ________ groggy
	36. ________ gross	42. ________ grip
	37. ________ grocer	43. ________ guess

Score the Practice exercise using the Answer Key in the back of this book, and go on to the Composition part of the guide.

Composition

This part of the guide will help you apply what you have learned about using the dictionary. Choose a short story to read from available book titles. Find **ten** words in the selection that you would like to know better. For each of these words do the following:

- Write the word in your notebook.
- Find the word in the dictionary and copy one of the definitions.
- Write a sentence which uses the word and conveys its meaning.

Use the Checklist to help you review and revise your writing.

Checklist	Yes	No
1. I selected ten words.	_____	_____
2. I wrote one dictionary definition for each word.	_____	_____
3. I wrote ten sentences that convey the meanings of the words I selected.	_____	_____
4. I proofread and edited my writing.	_____	_____
Proofread: to look for errors and indicate them.		
Edit: to revise your writing, if necessary.		
5. I wrote a corrected copy of my work.	_____	_____

Submit the completed writing assignment and Practice exercise to your instructor for evaluation.

3.

The Complete Sentence

This guide will help you to write complete sentences. Read each part of the Practice exercise and answer all **28** questions.

Practice

The following exercises will show you how to recognize and correct problem sentences.

The Fragment

A fragment is an incomplete sentence. When you read a fragment, you know that something is missing. For example:

The girl brushing her hair

This fragment can be made into a complete sentence in the following ways:

The girl is brushing her hair.

The girl brushing her hair is pretty.

I saw the girl brushing her hair.

Is the girl brushing her hair?

The two phrases below are fragments. In each, something is missing. Rewrite each fragment so that it is a complete sentence. A complete sentence expresses a complete thought.

The boy washing the car

The truck going too fast

1. ______________________________

2. ______________________________

The Run-on Sentence

A run-on sentence consists of many ideas all trying to fit into one complete sentence. It seems to go on forever, and the reader finds it hard to understand what the writer is trying to say.

Here is an example of a run-on sentence:

> On my way to work I got a flat tire but I couldn't change it myself so I tied a white cloth to the antenna and waited inside my car until finally a passing motorist stopped when he noticed the white cloth and offered to change the tire for me even though he was in a hurry he stopped because he is an individual who cares about other people.

In this passage there are far too many ideas to fit into one sentence. Three ways of correcting the run-on sentence are explained in the following exercises.

End Punctuation End punctuation is used to indicate the end of a complete sentence. Each of the following is an example of end puctuation.

the period (.)

the question mark (?)

the exclamation point (!)

The period (.) is used to end a complete sentence.

The question mark (?) is used to end a complete sentence that asks a question.

The exclamation point (!) is used to end a complete sentence that expresses a strong feeling.

Write the correct end punctuation for each of these sentences:

3. This morning I got a flat tire ______
4. How did you get the flat tire ______
5. Oh no! My car has another flat ______

The Conjunction The conjunction is a word that is used to connect two complete thoughts. Each of these is a conjunction: **and**, **but**, **or**. In the following sentence, two thoughts are connected by the conjunction *but*.

I would have helped change the tire, **but**
I didn't have time to stop.

Connect each pair of sentences below using the conjunction given. Remember to use a comma (,) before each conjunction.

and My car has a flat tire. I may have to walk to work.

6. ____

but I would have changed the tire. I didn't know how to do it.

7. ____

or Can you change the tire? Do you want to call the service station?

8. ____

The Semicolon A semicolon (;) is used to connect two related sentences when they are not joined by a conjunction. A semicolon can be used in place of a conjunction. The first word that follows a semicolon begins with a lower case (small) letter.

Conjunction	He cares about other people, **and** he always offers to help.
Semicolon	He cares about other people; he always offers to help.

Use a semicolon to connect each set of sentences below.

She waited by the side of the road. Many cars passed by without stopping.

9. ____

He saw a white cloth tied to the radio antenna. He knew she needed help.

10. ____

The man was kind. He changed the tire.

11. ____

Three Kinds of Complete Sentences

The Simple Sentence A simple sentence tells us **who** or **what** the sentence is about. Who or what (a person or a thing) is the subject of the sentence. A simple sentence also tells us what the subject **does**, or that **it exists** and **where it is**. Study the examples and answer questions 12 through 19.

Example The little girl pulled the cat's tail.

This simple sentence tells us who is doing what.

12. Who pulled the cat's tail? ______________________

13. What did the little girl do? ______________________

Example The bike races down the hill.

This simple sentence tells us what is doing what.

14. What races down the hill? ______________________

15. What does the bike do? ______________________

Example The ball is on the table.

This simple sentence tells us what is where.

16. What is on the table? ______________________

17. Where is the ball? ______________________

Example The boy is at the movies.

This simple sentence tells us who is where.

18. Who is at the movies? ______________________

19. Where is the boy? ______________________

The Compound Sentence A compound sentence is made of two simple sentences that are joined by a conjunction such as **and**, **but**, **or**. Each of the compound sentences that follow contains two simple sentences which are underlined. A comma is used before each conjunction.

The girl pulled the cat's tail, and the cat ran away.

She tried to pull the cat's tail, but the cat ran away.

Would she like a cat, or would she rather have a dog?

In exercises 20 through 22, do the following:

- Underline each of the two simple sentences.
- Circle the conjunction that connects these sentences.
- Place the comma where it belongs.

20. I can come to the party and I'll bring a cake.

____

21. I can help you with your work later but I want to rest now.

____

22. Do you want to eat at eleven or would you rather eat at twelve?

____

The Complex Sentence A complex sentence consists of a **subordinate clause** (a fragment) and a **main clause** (which can stand alone as a complete sentence). In other words, a complex sentence is made up of an incomplete thought and a complete thought joined together.

In each of the complex sentences below, the part that is underlined once is the subordinate clause (the fragment). It cannot stand alone. The part that is underlined twice is the main clause. It can stand alone as a complete sentence.

In these examples, the subordinate clause comes first and the main clause second; there is a comma in between.

If I plan ahead, I can achieve all my goals.

When you leave the room, please close the door quietly.

In exercises 23 through 25, underline the subordinate clause once and the main clause twice.

23. If my little sister stays home, I am going to the beach.

24. When I swim, I like to wear goggles.

25. While we're on vacation, my brother and I plan to go sailing.

When a complex sentence begins with a subordinate clause, you need to use a comma.

In each of the complex sentences below, the part that is underlined twice is the main clause. It can stand alone as a complete sentence. The part that is underlined once is the subordinate clause (the fragment). It cannot stand alone. In these examples, the main clause comes first and the subordinate clause second; no comma is needed.

I can achieve all my goals if I plan ahead.

Please close the door quietly when you leave the room.

In exercises 26 through 28 below, underline the main clause twice and the subordinate clause once.

26. I am going to the beach if my little sister stays home.

27. I like to wear goggles when I swim.

28. My brother and I plan to go sailing while we're on vacation.

You do not need to use a comma when a complex sentence begins with a main clause.

Score the Practice exercise using the Answer Key, and go on to the Composition part of this guide.

Composition

This part of the guide will help you apply what you have learned about writing complete sentences. Read the run-on sentence that follows.

On my way to work I got a flat tire but I couldn't change it myself so I tied a white cloth to the antenna and waited inside my car until finally a passing motorist stopped when he noticed the white cloth and offered to change the tire for me even though he was in a hurry he stopped because he is an individual who cares about other people.

Follow the steps outlined here to correct the run-on sentence.

- Rewrite the passage so that it contains complete sentences that present all of the writer's ideas.
- Use any of the ways you have learned, alone or in combination, to correct the run-on sentence. You may want to add or eliminate some words.

Use the Checklist to help you review and revise your writing. Do this for all drafts and your final copy.

Checklist	**Yes**	**No**
1. I rewrote the passage so that it contains only complete sentences.	_____	_____
2. I used capital letters to begin each sentence.	_____	_____
3. I used proper end punctuation for each sentence.	_____	_____
4. I used commas and conjunctions to combine my ideas.	_____	_____
5. I used the semicolon to connect two sentences that are closely related in thought.	_____	_____
6. I proofread and edited my writing.	_____	_____

Proofread: to look for errors and indicate them.

Edit: to revise your writing, if necessary.

7. I wrote a corrected copy of my work.	_____	_____

Submit the completed writing assignment and Practice exercise to your instructor for evaluation.

4.

Answering Questions

This guide will help you to answer questions clearly and completely. Answering questions in writing can prove to be a very valuable skill in school, at work, and in your personal correspondence. There are **three** important rules to remember when answering a question.

- Use complete sentences to answer the question.
- Restate the entire question in your answer so that the reader knows all parts of the question.
- Provide information from the reading selection. If the question is not based on a reading, draw on your own knowledge and experience to answer the question. You may want to use a reference source such as an encyclopedia.

Read the following passage from "The Scarlet Ibis," a short story by James Hurst. The story is about a boy and his sickly baby brother.

> When he was two, if you laid him on his stomach, he began to try to move himself, straining terribly. The doctor said that with his weak heart this strain would probably kill him, but it didn't. Trembling, he'd push himself up, turning first red, then a soft purple, and finally collapse back onto the bed like an old worn-out doll. I can still see Mama watching him, her hand pressed tight across her mouth, her eyes wide and unblinking. But he learned to crawl (it was his third winter), and we brought him out of the front bedroom, putting him on the rug before the fireplace. For the first time he became one of us.

Practice

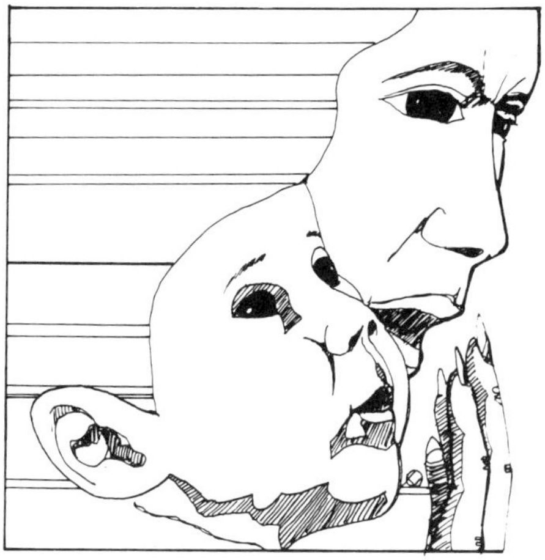

Read each part of the following exercise and answer all **18** questions. For each item, write either **yes** or **no**.

Question Why is the mother scared as she watches her baby straining to move?

Written below are three different answers to this question. Read each answer and complete the exercise that follows it.

Answer Because the doctor has said it would kill him.

1. ______ Is this answer a complete sentence?
2. ______ Does the answer restate the entire question?
3. ______ Does the answer provide information from the reading selection?

Answer The doctor said that the straining would kill him.

4. ______ Is this answer a complete sentence?
5. ______ Does the answer restate the entire question?
6. ______ Does the answer provide information from the reading selection?

Answer The mother is scared as she watches her baby straining to move, because the doctor has said that the strain on his weak heart would probably kill the child.

7. ______ Is this answer a complete sentence?

8. ______ Does the answer restate the entire question?

9. ______ Does the answer provide information from the reading selection?

In this next part there are three questions. Each is followed by a group of answers. Only one answer in each group conforms to the three rules for answering questions:

The answer is a complete sentence

The answer restates the entire question.

The answer provides information from the reading selection, or from your own knowledge and experience.

Write **yes** for those answers that comply with all three rules. Write **no** for those answers that do not comply with all three rules.

Question Why is the sky blue?

10. ______ Because of dust particles and water vapor in our atmosphere.

11. ______ It reflects only blue.

12. ______ The sky is blue because dust particles and water vapor in our atmosphere reflect only blue.

Question Why would someone say that a mirror is truthful?

13. ______ Someone would say that a mirror is truthful because it makes us see ourselves as we really are.

14. ______ Because it makes us see ourselves.

15. ______ It's truthful because it makes us see ourselves as we really are.

Question Why is ice cream delicious on a hot summer day?

16. ______ It tastes good and is so refreshing.

17. ______ Because it's so refreshing.

18. ______ Ice cream is delicious on a hot summer day because it tastes good and is so refreshing.

Score the Practice exercise using the Answer Key, and go on to the Composition part of this guide.

Composition

This part of the guide will help you apply what you have learned about answering questions. Choose a fiction or nonfiction selection to read from available textbooks. Check to see that the selection is followed by *thought* or *review* questions about the reading. After you read the selection, do the following:

- Copy **five** questions and answer each, keeping in mind the three rules you have learned.

Use the Checklist to help you review and revise your writing. Do this for all drafts and your final copy.

Checklist	**Yes**	**No**
1. I selected five questions and answered all of them.	_____	_____
2. My answers conform to the three rules for answering questions.	_____	_____
3. I used capital letters to begin each sentence, and proper end punctuation.	_____	_____
4. I used commas and conjunctions to combine my ideas.	_____	_____
5. I proofread and edited my writing. **Proofread:** to look for errors and indicate them. **Edit:** to revise your writing, if necessary.	_____	_____
6. I wrote a corrected copy of my work.	_____	_____

Submit the completed writing assignment and Practice exercise to your instructor for evaluation.

5.

Transitional Words and Phrases

This guide will help you to use transitional words and phrases. **When you want to connect two ideas in writing, transitions act as links that hold your ideas together.** The links you wish to make in your writing depend on your purpose. Below are a series of exercises in which transitional words and phrases are used.

Practice

Read each part of the following exercise and answer all **28** questions.

Time Relationships

In a time relationship events can occur before, at the same time as, or after other events.

Example A rainbow appeared **after** the rain.

If your purpose is to show a time relationship, the words below will help you. Choose words from this list to fill in the blanks in the two paragraphs that follow.

after	eventually	later	soon
afterwards	finally	meanwhile	sooner
always	first	next	so that
as soon as	following	now	then
at the same time	immediately	once	today
before	in order to	second	until
during	in the meantime	someday	when
earlier	last	sometimes	

The alarm clock rings. ______________ I get out of bed. I prepare my clothes ______________ I wash up. I get dressed, and ______________ I eat breakfast. ______________ I'm ready to leave. Today looks like it's going to be a fine day.

1 2 3 4

Let's make dinner. ______________ make salad. ______________ broil the steaks. Don't let them burn. ______________ set the table. ______________ pour the wine. Enjoy!

5 6 7 8

Relationships Between Ideas

When you want to express two related thoughts about the same subject, you can connect them using transitions.

Example Today is a great day **because** I got the job I wanted.

If your purpose is to show a relationship between ideas, the words below will help you. Choose words from this list to fill in the blanks in the two paragraphs that follow.

accordingly	even though	mainly	similarly
also	furthermore	moreover	since
and	if	more important	therefore
as	in the same way	most important	unless
because	like	nevertheless	while
besides	likewise	otherwise	

You can make your dreams come true, ________ (9) you want them to. ________ (10) you are young, you can begin to make plans. You will succeed ________ (11) you have a direction and goals.

A good education and practical experience are often the keys to success. ________ (12) formal education is important, on the job experience is ________ (13) needed. You will be a more confident ________ (14) poised applicant ________ (15) you are sure of your skills.

Restating Main Ideas

When you restate an idea, you say the same thing another way.

Example The facts show that regular exercise is good for your health. **As a result**, millions of people have started jogging, swimming, and dancing.

If your purpose is to restate main ideas, the words below will help you. Choose words from this list to fill in the blanks in the two paragraphs that follow.

so	because of
hence	in conclusion
thus	as a result
due to	consequently
since	for this reason
evidently	as a result of
as long as	it is evident
summarily	in view of

Drinking and driving don't mix. ________________ (16) alcohol slows your reflexes and clouds your judgment, driving while drunk can be dangerous. ________________ (17) all of the alcohol related injuries and deaths, many states impose severe penalties for driving while intoxicated. ________________ (18), to protect your own life and the lives of others, drive sober.

The dollar buys less today ______________ (19) inflation. ______________ (20), people must buy carefully. ______________ (21), a penny saved is a penny earned.

Opposite Points of View

You can use transitions to connect two opposing ideas.

Example Travel by train is interesting, **but** flying is faster.

If your purpose is to express opposite points of view, the words below will help you. Choose words from this list to fill in the blanks in the two paragraphs that follow.

although	in contrast	the reverse	while
but	on the contrary	though	yet
conversely	on the other hand	unless	
however	than	unlike	

The thought of living on your own sounds exciting, ______________ (22) it may not be so easy to do. ______________ (23) the freedom of making your own choices is tempting, earning money and keeping a house can be difficult. Many young people think about living alone, ______________ (24) actually doing it requires a lot of planning. ______________ (25) you are really ready, think twice about going out on your own.

Sharing an apartment with others has both good and bad points. Sharing expenses can be a real advantage, __________ (26) only if people cooperate. It is comforting to have people around. __________ (27), there are times when you want to be alone. When you live by yourself, you don't have to be concerned with what your roommates think or feel. Don't plan to live with others __________ (28) you are prepared to make compromises.

There are other transitional words and phrases besides the ones mentioned here. All transitions act as links that connect ideas and create unity in your writing.

Score the Practice exercise using the Answer Key, and go on to Composition part of this guide.

Composition

This part of the guide will help you apply what you have learned about using transitional words and phrases. For each of the four exercises, follow these steps:

- Refer to the word lists in the Practice exercise to help you.
- Underline transitional words and phrases that you use in your writing.

1. Choose one topic and write **three** sentences that show time relationships.

Sunday morning	getting ready for a date
the end of the day	stages in a person's life

2. Choose one topic and write **three** sentences that show relationships between ideas.

after graduation	household chores
sharing feelings	old age

3. State the main idea of the topic you wrote about in exercise number two. Then write **two** sentences that restate this idea.

4. Choose one topic and write **three** sentences that express opposite points of view.

school prayer	teenage marriage
the drinking age	country vs. city living

Use the Checklist to help you review and revise your writing. Do this for all drafts and your final copy.

Checklist	**Yes**	**No**
1. I wrote three sentences that use transitional words and phrases to show time relationships.	_____	_____
2. I wrote three sentences that use transitional words and phrases to show relationships between ideas.	_____	_____
3. I wrote two sentences that use transitional words and phrases to restate a main idea.	_____	_____
4. I wrote three sentences that use transitional words and phrases to present opposite points of view.	_____	_____
5. I wrote complete sentences.	_____	_____
6. I used capital letters to begin each sentence, and proper end punctuation.	_____	_____
7. I proofread and edited my writing.	_____	_____

Proofread: to look for errors and indicate them.
Edit: to revise your writing, if necessary.

8. I wrote a corrected copy of my work.	_____	_____

Submit the completed writing assignment and Practice exercise to your instructor for evaluation.

6.

Sentence Combining

This guide will help you to combine sentences in your writing. Sentence combining is a way of presenting several ideas in one sentence. While ideas can be stated one by one in separate, short sentences (**kernels**), your writing will be more interesting and effective if you combine these sentences. As with transitional words and phrases, you can use sentence combining to connect ideas and create unity in your writing.

Practice

Read each part of the following exercise and answer all **22** questions. Begin with the model paragraph.

It is a Sunday afternoon in early autumn. The day is perfect for taking a stroll through the park. Leaves fall from the trees, covering the ground with many colors. A young couple hold hands as they walk by. Their sparkling eyes reflect the sun's brilliant rays. The day is like a painting that is alive with people and colors.

In the exercise that follows, the model paragraph is presented one sentence at a time. Each sentence is followed by a series of questions. Fill in each blank with a one word answer. As you do this, you will be making a kernel sentence. This exercise takes a sentence that contains several ideas and breaks it down into kernel sentences.

It is a Sunday afternoon in early autumn.

What day of the week is it?

1. It is ________________.

What time of day is it?

2. It is ________________.

What season of the year is it?

3. It is ________________.

What part of the season is it?

4. It is ________________ autumn.

Kernel sentences 1, 2, 3, and 4, when combined, make the first sentence of the paragraph.

The day is perfect for taking a stroll through the park.

What kind of day is it?

5. It is a ______________ day.

What is the day perfect for doing?

6. The day is perfect for taking a ______________.

Where does the stroll take place?

7. The stroll is through the ______________.

Kernel sentences 5, 6, and 7, when combined, make the second sentence of the paragraph.

Leaves fall from the trees, covering the ground with many colors.

What falls?

8. The ______________ fall.

Where do they fall from?

9. Leaves fall from the ______________.

What are the leaves doing to the ground.

10. The leaves are ______________ the ground.

How do the leaves differ from one another?

11. The leaves are of many ______________.

Kernel sentences 8, 9, 10, and 11, when combined, make the third sentence of the paragraph.

A young couple hold hands as they walk by.

Who walks by?

12. A ________________ walk by.

How old are they?

13. They are ________________.

What are they doing?

14. They are ________________ ________________.

Kernel sentences 12, 13, and 14, when combined, make the fourth sentence of the paragraph.

Their sparkling eyes reflect the sun's brilliant rays.

What kind of eyes do they have?

15. They have ________________ eyes.

What do their eyes reflect?

16. Their eyes reflect ________________.

Where are the rays from?

17. The rays are from the ________________.

What kind of rays are they?

18. They are ________________ rays.

Kernel sentences 15, 16, 17, and 18, when combined, make the fifth sentence of the paragraph.

The day is like a painting that is alive with people and colors.

What is the day like?

19. The day is like a _______________.

What is special about the painting?

20. This painting is _______________.

What is alive in the painting?

21. _______________ are alive in the painting.

What else is alive in the painting?

22. _______________ are alive in the painting.

Kernel sentences 19, 20, 21, and 22, when combined, make the last sentence of the paragraph.

Score the Practice exercise using the Answer Key, and go on to the Composition part of this guide.

Composition

This part of the guide will help you apply what you have learned about sentence combining. The two exercises that follow, "Table" and "Working Girl," are from the book *Sentence Combining* by William Strong. In each exercise, related kernel sentences are grouped together. Each group of sentences contains several ideas that can be combined into one sentence.

For each exercise, do the following:

- Underline the important information in each kernel sentence. The first one is done for you.
- Combine the underlined information in each group to form one sentence for that group.
- Write these sentences in sequence to form a paragraph.

TABLE

1. The table is littered with refuse.
   The refuse belongs to other people.

2. They have left signatures everywhere.
   The signatures are stained.
   The signatures are greasy.

3. He stares at cups.
   The cups are in a pile.
   The cups are for coffee.
   The cups are stained with lipstick.

4. Off to one side is a hamburger.
   The hamburger is half-eaten.
   Flies rest there.
   The flies are nervous.

5. A sign is buried in the garbage.
   The sign is small.
   The sign is neatly lettered.

6. He reads the sign.
   The sign pleads for students to bus their own dishes.

WORKING GIRL

1. Jan is a working girl.
   She bounces through a routine.
   The routine is from nine to five.

2. Then she waits for the bus.
   The bus takes her back.
   The bus takes her to her apartment.
   The apartment is uptown.

3. She is now on her own.
   She is having a great time.

4. Her senses are alive to something.
   The something is new.
   The something is delicious.
   The something is called "freedom."

5. Each day is electric.
   Each day is exciting.

6. Her face is poised.
   Her face is proud.
   Her face smiles with confidence.
   The confidence is quiet.

7. She has legs.
   Her legs are long.
   Her legs are waxy.

8. She has dates.
   The dates are many.
   But she is in no hurry.
   The hurry would be to settle down.

Use the Checklist to help you review and revise your writing. Do this for all drafts and your final copy.

Checklist	**Yes**	**No**
1. I underlined the important information in each kernel sentence.	____	____
2. I combined information in each group to form one sentence.	____	____
3. I wrote a series of complete sentences that form a paragraph. I wrote one paragraph for "Table" and another for "Working Girl."	____	____
4. I used capital letters to begin each sentence, and proper end punctuation.	____	____
5. I proofread and edited my writing.	____	____

Proofread: to look for errors and indicate them.
Edit: to revise your writing, if necessary.

6. I wrote a corrected copy of my work.	____	____

Submit the completed writing assignment and Practice exercise to your instructor for evaluation.

Tea

II.
The Paragraph

In this section you will build on your sentence skills by writing paragraphs. The first guide, Paragraph Development, presents the basic structure of the paragraph.

Other guides teach different ways of writing one-paragraph compositions. The last guide in this section, The Three Paragraph Essay, is a bridge between writing paragraphs and writing longer compositions.

Guides

7.

Paragraph Development: A

This guide will help you to write a paragraph. A paragraph is composed of three parts:

a topic sentence

supporting details

a concluding sentence

Practice

Read each part of the following exercise and answer all **17** questions. Begin by reading the model paragraph.

> Anyone can build a campfire. You begin with some wood shavings or small dry twigs. On top of that you place some larger twigs or thin branches. When you begin to pile on the heavier wooden pieces, use a crisscross pattern. This leaves plenty of space for the fire to come through. Light the wood shavings or dried twigs with a match, and the job is done. There is nothing complicated about building a campfire.

The **topic sentence** tells the reader what the paragraph is about. It is usually the first sentence. Copy the topic sentence of the paragraph.

1. ____

Supporting details provide facts, examples, and descriptions that relate to the topic of the paragraph. Copy each sentence that presents facts, examples, or descriptions about how to build a campfire.

2. ____

3. ____

4. ____

5. ____

6. ____

The **concluding sentence** summarizes the topic of the paragraph for the reader. Copy the last sentence of the paragraph.

7. ____

Read the following paragraph:

> When I was little, my older sister was always trying to scare me. One night she hid near the bottom of the staircase. As I walked by, she jumped out at me and let loose a loud, bloodcurdling scream. Another time I asked her to tell me a bedtime story. Holding a small flashlight under her chin, she turned the lights off, lowered her voice to a whisper, and opened her eyes wide. I was terrified and she hadn't even started the story! Her tales of ghosts and monsters kept me shivering with fright long after she left the room. Now, I laugh whenever I recall how easily my sister could scare me when I was young.

Copy the topic sentence of the paragraph.

8. ____

List **three** ways the older sister scared the young child. These are the supporting details for the topic of the paragraph.

9. ______________________________

10. ______________________________

11. ______________________________

Copy the concluding sentence of the paragraph.

12. ______________________________

Read the following paragraph:

> When I looked through our family photo album last Sunday, I was reminded of all the good times we had during our summer vacations. There were several photos of Dad and me in a boat, holding our prize catches for the day. I saw five pictures I took of my sister learning to water ski. Most of the time she was in the water. The funniest picture was a closeup of my family as we rode the Water Flume at an amusement park. Mom looked as if she were about to be shot. The photographer knew exactly when to snap that one! Summer vacations are great because I always have a wonderful time.

Copy the topic sentence of the paragraph

13. ____________________

List **three** different vacation activities mentioned in the paragraph. These are the supporting details for the topic of this paragraph.

14. ____________________

15. ____________________

16. ____________________

Copy the concluding sentence of the paragraph.

17. ____________________

Score the Practice exercise using the Answer Key, and go on to the Composition part of this guide.

Composition

This part of the guide will help you apply what you have learned about writing a paragraph. Choose **one** topic and write a paragraph. Follow the plan outlined below.

Topics

If I had only a year to live . . .

The best friend I ever had . . .

I was once punished for . . .

When I was little, I was really afraid of . . .

The funniest experience I ever had . . .

Plan

- Indent to indicate the beginning of the paragraph. Introduce your topic in the first sentence.
- Write at least **five** sentences that contain supporting details: facts, examples, and descriptions that relate to the topic.
- Write a concluding statement that summarizes the topic of the paragraph for the reader.

Use the Checklist to help you review and revise your writing. Do this for all drafts and your final copy.

Checklist	Yes	No
1. I indented to begin my paragraph.	_____	_____
2. I introduced my topic in the first sentence.	_____	_____
3. I wrote at least five sentences that contain supporting details for my topic.	_____	_____
4. The last sentence of the paragraph summarizes the topic for the reader.	_____	_____
5. I used transitions to connect ideas and create unity in my writing.	_____	_____
6. I wrote complete sentences that begin with capital letters, and used proper end punctuation.	_____	_____
7. I proofread and edited my composition.	_____	_____
8. I wrote a corrected copy of my work.	_____	_____

Submit the completed writing assignment and Practice exercise to your instructor for evaluation.

8.

Paragraph Development: B

The first part of this guide gives you an opportunity to practice your grammar, usage, and punctuation. It can also be used to improve your spelling, learn new words, and sharpen your reading comprehension skills. These activities will help to improve your writing.

Skills Practice

Choose one or more of the following exercises and answer at least **thirty** questions:

A **corrective** exercise recommended by your instructor.

A **spelling** exercise from available materials.

A **vocabulary** exercise from available materials.

A **reading comprehension** exercise from available materials.

Record the number of questions you complete, and score the exercise using available answer keys. Then go on to the Composition part of this guide.

Composition

This section of the guide provides additional practice in writing a paragraph. Choose a fiction or nonfiction selection to read from available book titles. Write a paragraph based on your reading by following the plan below.

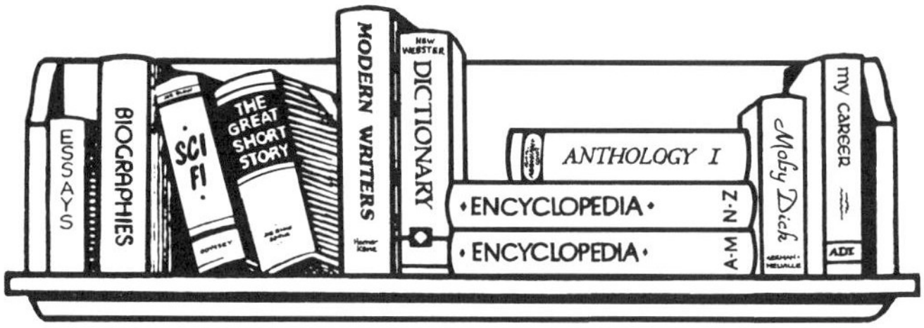

Plan

- Write the name of the selection and the main point the author is making (the theme). This is your topic sentence.
- Write at least **five** sentences that support your topic sentence. Present details from the selection: facts, examples, and descriptions.
- Conclude your paragraph with a sentence that summarizes the topic of the paragraph for the reader.

Use the Checklist to help you review and revise your writing. Do this for all drafts and your final copy.

Checklist	**Yes**	**No**
1. I indented to begin my paragraph.	_____	_____
2. In my topic sentence, I wrote the title and stated the theme of the selection.	_____	_____
3. I wrote at least five sentences that contain supporting details for the topic.	_____	_____
4. The last sentence of the paragraph summarizes the topic for the reader.	_____	_____
5. I used transitions to connect ideas and create unity in my writing.	_____	_____
6. I wrote complete sentences that begin with capital letters, and used proper end punctuation.	_____	_____
7. I proofread and edited my compostion.	_____	_____
8. I wrote a corrected copy of my work.	_____	_____

Submit the completed writing assignment and Practice exercise to your instructor for evaluation.

9.

The Narrative Paragraph: A

This guide will help you to write a narrative paragraph. **A narrative tells a story.** The model paragraph is from "An Ornery Kind of Kid," a short story by William Saroyan.

Practice

Read each part of the following exercise and answer all **13** questions. Begin by reading the paragraph.

> It was getting dark fast by then, and there didn't seem to be anything alive around at all, so he began to shoot the gun just to get used to it. Pretty soon he could shoot it and not get knocked down. He kept shooting and walking, and finally it was dark and it seemed he was lost. He stumbled over a hidden rock and fell and shot the gun by accident and got a lot of dirt in his eyes. He got up and almost cried, but he managed not to, and then he found a road, but he had no idea where it went or which direction to take. He was scratched and sore all over and not very happy about the way he'd shot the gun by accident. He was scared, too, and he said a prayer a minute and meant every word of what he said. And he understood for the first time in his life why people liked to go to church.

The author begins by creating the setting. The setting tells the reader the **time** and **place** of the story. He then tells what happens to a specific character. We can use all the information in the paragraph to make inferences (draw conclusions) in answering the questions.

1. Use the dictionary to find the definition of the word *ornery.*

   ____

2. What time of day is it?

   ____

3. What words in the paragraph help you to draw this conclusion?

   ____

4. Where does the story take place?

   ____

5. What words in the paragraph help you to draw this conclusion?

   ____

6. Is the author writing about an adult or a young person?

____

7. What words in the paragraph help you to draw this conclusion?

____

8. What is the character doing?

____

9. What words in the paragraph help you to draw this conclusion.

____

10. How does the character feel?

____

11. What words in the paragraph help you to draw this conclusion?

____

12. How does the character in this paragraph console himself?

____

13. What words in the paragraph help you to draw this conclusion?

____

Score the exercise using the Answer Key, and go on to the Composition part of this guide.

Composition

This part of the guide will help you apply what you have learned about writing a narrative paragraph. Choose **one** topic and list, in chronological order, the things that happened. Use this list as you follow the plan for writing a narrative paragraph.

Topics

The first time I went on a date.

The first time I took a ride on a rollercoaster.

The first time I traveled alone.

The last time I had an accident.

The last time I got blamed, and it wasn't my fault.

Plan

- Begin your paragraph by creating the setting. The setting tells the reader the time and place of the story.
- You are the narrator of this story. Tell who you are and what is happening in the story. Choose your details carefully, using words that create a picture for the reader. Write at least **five** sentences for this part.
- Write **two** sentences to end your paragraph. Tell the reader **how** you feel about the outcome, and **why** you feel this way.

Use the Checklist to help you review and revise your writing. Do this for all drafts and your final copy.

Checklist	**Yes**	**No**
1. Before I began my paragraph, I listed the things that happened in chronological order.	____	____
2. I began the paragraph by creating the setting.	____	____
3. I told what happened, in detail. I wrote at least five sentences for this part.	____	____
4. In my concluding sentences, I expressed my feelings about the outcome.	____	____
5. I used transitions to connect ideas and create unity in my writing.	____	____
6. I wrote complete sentences that begin with capital letters, and used proper end punctuation.	____	____
7. I proofread and edited my composition.	____	____
8. I wrote a corrected copy of my work.	____	____

Submit the completed writing assignment and Practice exercise to your instructor for evaluation.

10.

The Narrative Paragraph: B

The first part of this guide gives you an opportunity to practice your grammar, usage, and punctuation. It can also be used to improve your spelling, learn new words, and sharpen your reading comprehension skills. These activities will help to improve your writing.

Skills Practice

Choose one or more of the following exercises and answer at least **thirty** questions:

A **corrective** exercise recommended by your instructor.

A **spelling** exercise from available materials.

A **vocabulary** exercise from available materials.

A **reading comprehension** exercise from available materials.

Record the number of questions you complete, and score the exercise using available answer keys. Then go on to the Composition part of this guide.

Composition

This section of the guide provides additional practice in writing a narrative paragraph. Choose a short story to read from available book titles. Select one character from the story and pretend you are that person. Then, list the events in chronological order that have happened to you. Use this list as you follow the plan for writing a narrative paragraph.

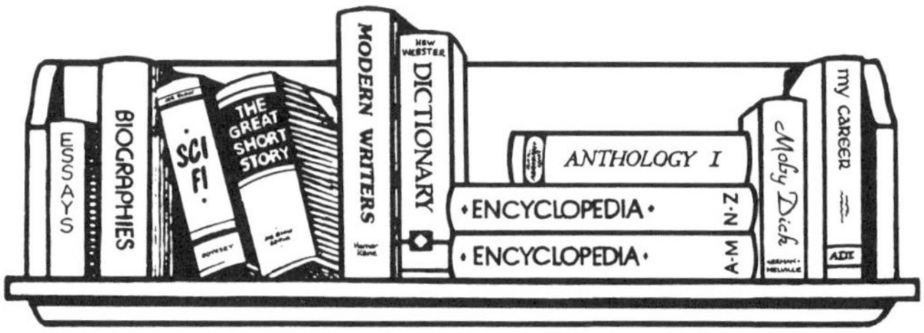

Plan

- Create the setting by telling the time and place of the story.
- Choose one character from the story and pretend you are that person. Let the reader know who you are.
- Tell what has happened in the story, and to whom. Choose your details carefully, using words that create a picture for the reader. Write at least **five** sentences for this part.
- Write **two** sentences to end your paragraph. Tell the reader **how** you feel about the outcome, and **why** you feel this way.

Use the Checklist to help you review and revise your writing. Do this for all drafts and your final copy.

Checklist	**Yes**	**No**
1. Before I began my paragraph, I listed the things that happened in chronological order.	____	____
2. I tell who I am and the time and place of the story.	____	____
3. I told what has happened in the story and to whom. I wrote at least five sentences for this part.	____	____
4. In my concluding sentences, I expressed my feelings about the outcome.	____	____
5. I used transitions to connect ideas and create unity in my writing.	____	____
6. I wrote complete sentences that begin with capital letters, and used proper end punctuation.	____	____
7. I proofread and edited my composition.	____	____
8. I wrote a corrected copy of my work.	____	____

Submit the completed writing assignment and Practice exercise to your instructor for evaluation.

11.

The Descriptive Paragraph: A

This guide will help you to write a descriptive paragraph. Description is used to create impressions that are vivid, real, and lifelike for the reader.

The writer appeals to the **five senses** by telling us how something **looks**, **tastes**, **smells**, **sounds**, and **feels**. These are five ways of describing a person, place, thing, or idea.

Practice

Read the model paragraph from "A Sound of Thunder" by Ray Bradbury, and answer all **45** questions.

> It came on great oiled striding legs. It towered thirty feet above half the trees, a great evil god. Each lower leg was a piston, a thousand pounds of white bone and thick ropes of muscle. Each thigh was a ton of meat. And from the upper body two delicate arms dangled out front with hands that might pick up men like toys. The snake neck coiled. Its mouth hung open showing a row of teeth like daggers. Its eyes rolled. They showed nothing but hunger. It closed its mouth in a death grin.

The sentences below are from the model paragraph that describes a monster. Each sentence is followed by a list of the five senses, the ways in which we know the world. Write the word(s) from each sentence next to the sensory category to which they belong. If no words from the sentence fit the category, write the word *none.* The first one is done for you.

It came on great oiled striding legs.

sight: **great oiled striding legs**

taste: **none**

smell: **none**

sound: **striding legs**

touch: **oiled**

It towered thirty feet above half the trees, a great evil god.

1. sight: ____________________
2. taste: ____________________
3. smell: ____________________
4. sound: ____________________
5. touch: ____________________

Each lower leg was a piston, a thousand pounds of white bone and thick ropes of muscle.

6. sight: ______________________________
7. taste: ______________________________
8. smell: ______________________________
9. sound: ______________________________
10. touch: ______________________________

Each thigh was a ton of meat.

11. sight: ______________________________
12. taste: ______________________________
13. smell: ______________________________
14. sound: ______________________________
15. touch: ______________________________

And from the upper body two delicate arms dangled out front with hands that might pick up men like toys.

16. sight: ______________________________
17. taste: ______________________________
18. smell: ______________________________
19. sound: ______________________________
20. touch: ______________________________

The snake neck coiled.

21. sight: ______________________________

22. taste: ______________________________

23. smell: ______________________________

24. sound: ______________________________

25. touch: ______________________________

Its mouth hung open showing a row of teeth like daggers.

26. sight: ______________________________

27. taste: ______________________________

28. smell: ______________________________

29. sound: ______________________________

30. touch: ______________________________

Its eyes rolled.

31. sight: ______________________________

32. taste: ______________________________

33. smell: ______________________________

34. sound: ______________________________

35. touch: ______________________________

They showed nothing but hunger.

36. sight: ______________________________

37. taste: ______________________________

38. smell: ______________________________

39. sound: ______________________________

40. touch: ______________________________

It closed its mouth in a death grin.

41. sight: ______________________________

42. taste: ______________________________

43. smell: ______________________________

44. sound: ______________________________

45. touch: ______________________________

Appealing primarily to the sense of sight, Ray Bradbury has created very vivid impressions for the reader. In general, it is easier to do this if you appeal to as many of the five senses as you can.

Score the exercise using the Answer Key, and go on to the Composition part of this guide.

Composition

This part of the guide will help you apply what you have learned about writing a descriptive paragraph. Choose **one** topic and list the ways in which your subject appeals to each of the five senses. Use this list as you follow the plan for writing a descriptive paragraph.

Topics

A dream car

A rock concert

A birthday party

A beautiful sunrise

An outrageous person

Plan

- In the first sentence introduce the person, place, thing, or idea your paragraph is about.
- Write at least **five** sentences in which you describe your subject as completely as possible. Appeal to as many senses as you can: sight, taste, smell, hearing, and touch. The actions of your subject may also be described.
- Write a concluding sentence that uses description to summarize the topic.

Use the Checklist to help you review and revise your writing. Do this for all drafts and your final copy.

Checklist	**Yes**	**No**
1. Before I began my paragraph, I listed the ways in which my subject appeals to each of the five senses.	_____	_____
2. In the first sentence I introduced the person, place, thing, or idea my paragraph is about.	_____	_____
3. I described my subject by appealing to the senses. (Check [✓] those that apply):	_____	_____
sight ____ taste ____ smell ____		
sound ____ touch ____		
4. I wrote at least five sentences of description.	_____	_____
5. I wrote a concluding sentence that contains description.	_____	_____
6. I used transitions to connect ideas and create unity in my writing.	_____	_____
7. I wrote complete sentences that begin with capital letters, and used proper end punctuation.	_____	_____
8. I proofread and edited my composition.	_____	_____
9. I wrote a corrected copy of my work.	_____	_____

Submit the completed writing assignment and Practice exercise to your instructor for evaluation.

12.

The Descriptive Paragraph: B

The first part of this guide gives you an opportunity to practice your grammar, usage, and punctuation. It can also be used to improve your spelling, learn new words, and sharpen your reading comprehension skills. These activities will help to improve your writing.

Skills Practice

Choose one or more of the following exercises and answer at least **thirty** questions:

A **corrective** exercise recommended by your instructor.

A **spelling** exercise from available materials.

A **vocabulary** exercise from available materials.

A **reading comprehension** exercise from available materials.

Record the number of questions you complete, and score the exercise using available answer keys. Then go on to the Composition part of this guide.

Composition

This section of the guide provides additional practice in writing a descriptive paragraph. Read a fiction or nonfiction selection from available book titles. Choose a subject to write about: a person, place, thing, or idea that appears in the selection. List the ways in which your subject appeals to each of the five senses. Use this list as you follow the plan for writing a descriptive paragraph.

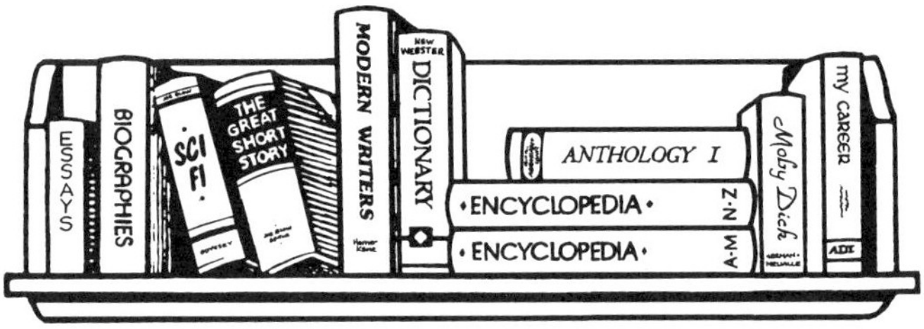

Plan

- In the first sentence introduce the person, place, thing, or idea your paragraph is about.
- Write at least **five** sentences in which you describe your subject as completely as possible. Appeal to as many senses as you can: sight, taste, smell, hearing, and touch. The actions of your subject may also be described.
- Write a concluding sentence that uses description to summarize the topic.

Use the Checklist to help you review and revise your writing. Do this for all drafts and your final copy.

Checklist	**Yes**	**No**
1. Before I began my paragraph, I listed the ways in which my subject appeals to each of the five senses.	____	____
2. In the first sentence I introduced the person, place, thing, or idea my paragraph is about.	____	____
3. I described my subject by appealing to the senses. (Check [✓] those that apply): sight ____ taste ____ smell ____ hearing ____ touch ____	____	____
4. I wrote at least five sentences of description.	____	____
5. I wrote a concluding sentence that contains description.	____	____
6. I used transitions to connect ideas and create unity in my writing.	____	____
7. I wrote complete sentences that begin with capital letters, and used proper end punctuation.	____	____
8. I proofread and edited my composition.	____	____
9. I wrote a corrected copy of my work.	____	____

Submit the completed writing assignment and Practice exercise to your instructor for evaluation.

13.

The Expository Paragraph: A

This guide will help you to write an expository paragraph. **Exposition** is writing that **explains facts and ideas** so that they are easily understood. You can use expository writing to:

- give directions about how to do something or how to get somewhere.
- explain why something is the way it is.
- write about a person, place, or event, as you might in a research report.

Practice

Read each part of the following exercise and answer all **23** questions.

The sentences on the following page are from the book, *Modern Spearfishing,* by I.S. Ivanovic. The sentences have been rearranged so that they are not in the right sequence. In the correct order, these sentences form an expository paragraph. The author uses exposition to give directions about how to prepare for spearfishing.

Reorganize the sentences that follow, *A* through *I*, to form a paragraph that clearly explains how one prepares to go spearfishing. First, look for the topic sentence. Next, look for transitional words which serve as clues to the order of the sentences.

Write a **number** next to each sentence to indicate its correct order in the paragraph. For example, write the number 1 next to the sentence which should come first in the paragraph. Use the numbers 2 through 9 to order the remaining sentences.

_____ A. Then place the gun near the edge of the water so that you can pick it up on your way in.

_____ B. You will find it best to make the flippers wet before you try to put them on.

_____ C. Once the goggles are on and your breathing tube is in your mouth, you are ready to go into the water.

_____ D. Put your ear plugs into your ears and put your rubber bathing cap on if you have one.

_____ E. I have found that the following sequence of preparatory steps for spearfishing has proved to be the most useful, although every fisherman develops his own way very soon.

_____ F. The next thing to do is to sit down on the ground, keeping as near to the edge of the water as you can, and then put on your flippers.

_____ G. Then tie your fish ring to your belt so that it is always on your left flank.

_____ H. When you have done that, put your glove on and then you are ready to prepare the mask or the goggles by making sure a mist will not form on the inside of the glass.

_____ I. First of all, load your gun, apply the safety catch if there is one, check your reel, and check the position of your line.

Now that you have reordered the sentences, write them in your notebook in paragraph form. Compare your work with the model that appears at the end of the Practice exercise.

In the topic sentence, the author gives you information about the **content** and **form** of his paragraph.

10. Content refers to the subject that is discussed. What is the subject of this paragraph? ______________________

11. The form tells us how the paragraph will be organized. How does the author propose to present the information?

    ____

12. How many different steps does the author use in explaining how to prepare for spearfishing? ______________

13. How many different transitional words and phrases does the author use in this paragraph to go from one step to the next? ______________________________

Write **ten** transitions used in the expository paragraph.

14. ______________	19. ______________
15. ______________	20. ______________
16. ______________	21. ______________
17. ______________	22. ______________
18. ______________	23. ______________

from MODERN SPEARFISHING

I have found that the following sequence of preparatory steps for spearfishing has proved to be the most useful, although every fisherman develops his own way very soon. First of all, load your gun, apply the safety catch if there is one, check your reel, and check the position of your line. Then place the gun near the edge of the water so that you can pick it up on your way in. Put your ear plugs into your ears and put your rubber bathing cap on if you have one. The next thing to do is to sit down on the ground, keeping as near to the edge of the water as you can, and then put on your flippers. You will find it best to make the flippers wet before you try to put them on. Then tie your fish ring to your belt so that it is always on your left flank. When you have done that, put your glove on and then you are ready to prepare the mask or the goggles by making sure a mist will not form on the inside of the glass. Once the goggles are on and your breathing tube is in your mouth, you are ready to go into the water.

Score the Practice exercise using the Answer Key, and go on to the Composition part of this guide.

Composition

This part of the guide will help you apply what you have learned about writing an expository paragraph. Choose **one** topic and list at least five steps, in order, that explain a process. Use this list as you follow the plan for writing an expository paragraph.

You may find it helpful to use reference sources such as the dictionary, encyclopedia, or other books. When you use information from reference sources, do not copy directly from the book. Always use your own words to rephrase what you have read.

Topics

Changing a tire

How a rainbow forms

Making a super banana split

Getting to work or school from where you live

The Wright brothers' first flight

Plan

- Write a topic sentence that introduces your subject (content) and tells how the information will be presented (form).
- Write at least **five** sentences in which you explain your subject as completely as possible.
- Write a conclusion for your paragraph that summarizes the topic for the reader.

Use the Checklist to help you review and revise your writing. Do this for all drafts and your final copy.

Checklist	Yes	No
1. Before I began my paragraph, I listed at least five steps that explain a process.	____	____
2. I wrote a topic sentence that introduces my subject and tells how I plan to present the information.	____	____
3. Using my own words, I wrote at least five sentences in which I explain my subject to the reader.	____	____
4. I wrote a conclusion that summarizes my topic for the reader.	____	____
5. I used transitions to connect ideas and create unity in my writing.	____	____
6. I wrote complete sentences that begin with capital letters, and used proper end punctuation.	____	____
7. I proofread and edited my composition.	____	____
8. I wrote a corrected copy of my work.	____	____

Submit the completed writing assignment and Practice exercise to your instructor for evaluation.

14.

The Expository Paragraph: B

The first part of this guide gives you an opportunity to practice your grammar, usage, and punctuation. It can also be used to improve your spelling, learn new words, and sharpen your reading comprehension skills. These activities will help to improve your writing.

Skills Practice

Choose one or more of the following exercises and answer at least **thirty** questions:

A **corrective** exercise recommended by your instructor.

A **spelling** exercise from available materials.

A **vocabulary** exercise from available materials.

A **reading comprehension** exercise from available materials.

Record the number of questions you complete, and score the exercise using available answer keys. Then go on to the Composition part of this guide.

Composition

This section of the guide provides additional practice in writing an expository paragraph. Read a nonfiction selection from available book titles. Choose a process or event and list at least five steps, in order, that explain what happens. Use this list as you follow the plan for writing an expository paragraph. If you use reference sources, do not copy directly from the book. Use your own words to rephrase what you have read.

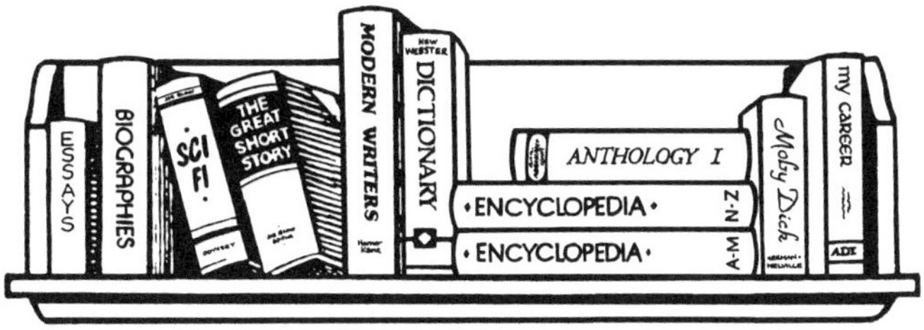

Plan

- Write a topic sentence that introduces your subject (content) and tells how the information will be presented (form).
- Write at least **five** sentences in which you explain your subject as completely as possible.
- Write a conclusion for your paragraph that summarizes the topic for the reader.

Use the Checklist to help you review and revise your writing. Do this for all drafts and your final copy.

Checklist	Yes	No
1. Before I began my paragraph, I listed at least five steps that explain a process.	_____	_____
2. I wrote a topic sentence that introduces my subject and tells how I plan to present the information.	_____	_____
3. Using my own words, I wrote at least five sentences in which I explain my subject to the reader.	_____	_____
4. I wrote a conclusion that summarizes my topic for the reader.	_____	_____
5. I used transitions to connect ideas and create unity in my writing.	_____	_____
6. I wrote complete sentences that begin with capital letters, and used proper end punctuation.	_____	_____
7. I proofread and edited my composition.	_____	_____
8. I wrote a corrected copy of my work.	_____	_____

Submit the completed writing assignment and Practice exercise to your instructor for evaluation.

15.

Using Examples: A

This guide will help you to write a paragraph using examples. **When you give an example, you point out something that is representative of a category.** The United States of America is an example of the category, *country.* Florida is an example of the category, *state.*

Practice

Read each part of this exercise and answer all **16** questions. The following paragraph is an excerpt from the nonfiction article, "As I Saw the U.S.A." Jan Morris, a British writer, uses examples to illustrate the behavior of Americans.

> Few Americans will walk anywhere if they can help it, either for practical purpose or for pleasure. You can do your banking from your car, without leaving the driving seat, by choosing a bank with a "curbside teller." You can post your letters in postboxes that protrude to the level of your car window. You can watch a film from your car in a "drive-in" cinema. At many stores you can be served in your car. At innumerable restaurants waitresses will hitch trays to the car door, so that you can eat without moving. In Florida there is even a "drive-in" church. There is no more characteristic gesture of American life than the casual rolling-down of a car window and the emergence of a hand, to grasp a hot dog or a theater ticket, a pound of apples or an evening paper, a check book or a soft drink from a roadside stall.

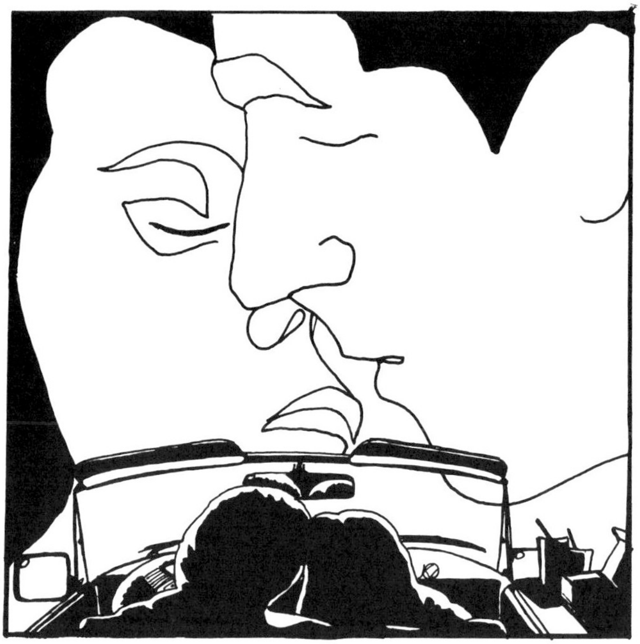

Write the topic sentence of this paragraph.

1. ____

The author uses examples to portray how Americans use their cars, rather than their legs, to go places and do things. List these examples below.

2. ______________________ 5. ______________________

3. ______________________ 6. ______________________

4. ______________________ 7. ______________________

In her concluding statement, the author uses more examples to summarize her point of view. Another way of summarizing this paragraph is to write a sentence that restates the point of view first expressed in the topic sentence.

Example It seems that Americans would rather drive than walk.

WORD LIST

angry	disco	Mercedes	scared
aunt	Earth	movie	soccer
basketball	excited	museum	spring
brother	fall	pizza	summer
cheeseburger	Ford	Pluto	tacos
concert	golf	purple	tennis
Corvette	grandmother	sailboat	Toyota
cousin	lipstick	salad	twelve
delighted	Mars	Saturn	winter

Each of the words in the list above is an example of a specific category. Write each word next to its appropriate category.

CATEGORIES

8. cars: ____________________
9. entertainment: ____________________
10. feelings: ____________________
11. food: ____________________
12. planets: ____________________
13. relatives: ____________________
14. seasons: ____________________
15. sports: ____________________
16. other: ____________________

Score the Practice exercise using the Answer Key, and go on to the Composition part of this guide.

Composition

This part of the guide will help you to apply what you have learned about writing a paragraph using examples. Each of the topics below can be used as an introduction to an illustrative paragraph. Before you begin your composition, list examples for the category you have chosen to illustrate. Use this list as you follow the plan for writing a paragraph using examples.

Topics

All kinds of people ride subways and buses.

Summer is a wonderful time of year.

A job is important in many ways.

You can tell a lot about a person by the way he or she eats.

There are many ways to travel.

Plan

- Introduce your topic in the first sentence of the paragraph.
- Write at least **five** sentences containing examples that illustrate the topic.
- Write a concluding sentence that summarizes what you have written.

Use the Checklist to help you review and revise your writing. Do this for all drafts and your final copy.

Checklist	**Yes**	**No**
1. Before I began my paragraph, I listed examples for the category (topic) I chose.	____	____
2. I introduced the topic in the first sentence of the paragraph.	____	____
3. I wrote five sentences which contain examples that illustrate the topic.	____	____
4. The last sentence of the paragraph summarizes what I have written.	____	____
5. I used transitions to connect ideas and create unity in my writing.	____	____
6. I wrote complete sentences that begin with capital letters, and used proper end punctuation.	____	____
7. I proofread and edited my composition.	____	____
8. I wrote a corrected copy of my work.	____	____

Submit the completed writing assignment and Practice exercise to your instructor for evaluation.

16.

Using Examples: B

The first part of this guide gives you an opportunity to practice your grammar, usage, and punctuation. It can also be used to improve your spelling, learn new words, and sharpen your reading comprehension skills. These activities will help to improve your writing.

Skills Practice

Choose one or more of the following exercises and answer at least **thirty** questions:

A **corrective** exercise recommended by your instructor.

A **spelling** exercise from available materials.

A **vocabulary** exercise from available materials.

A **reading comprehension** exercise from available materials.

Record the number of questions you complete, and score the exercise using available answer keys. Then go on to the Composition part of this guide.

Composition

This section of the guide provides additional practice in writing a paragraph using examples. Read a nonfiction selection from available book titles. Choose a category (topic) for which you can readily provide examples, and make a list of these examples. Use this list as you follow the plan for writing an illustrative paragraph.

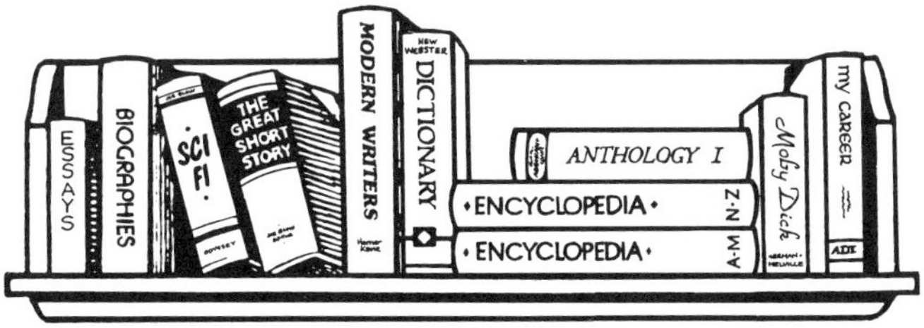

Plan

- Introduce your topic in the first sentence of the paragraph.
- Write at least **five** sentences containing examples that illustrate the topic.
- Write a concluding sentence that summarizes what you have written.

Use the Checklist to help your review and revise your writing. Do this for all drafts and your final copy.

Checklist	**Yes**	**No**
1. Before I began my paragraph, I listed examples for the category (topic) I chose.	_____	_____
2. I introduced the topic in the first sentence of the paragraph.	_____	_____
3. I wrote at least five sentences which contain examples that illustrate the topic.	_____	_____
4. The last sentence of the paragraph summarizes what I have written.	_____	_____
5. I used transitions to connect ideas and create unity in my writing.	_____	_____
6. I wrote complete sentences that begin with capital letters, and used proper end punctuation.	_____	_____
7. I proofread and edited my composition.	_____	_____
8. I wrote a corrected copy of my work.	_____	_____

Submit the completed writing assignment and Practice exercise to your instructor for evaluation.

17.

Using Definition: A

This guide will help you to write a paragraph using definition. The definition of a person, place, thing, or idea involves both description and explanation. While description appeals to the senses and is used by the writer to create impressions, **definition presents facts about the subject**.

Practice

Read each part of the following exercise and answer all **19** questions.

When you buy land, it must be surveyed. A survey defines the limits and boundaries of your property and what it contains. In the same way, **definition explains** your subject to your audience **in very concrete terms**. In the following paragraph, the writer uses concrete terms to define the subject.

> The guitar is a handheld, stringed, musical instrument made of wood. The **body** of the guitar is like a box that has a flat front and back, and is hollow inside. The shape is that of a pear or a figure eight. The circular opening on the front of the guitar is called the **sound hole**. A long piece of wood, the **finger board**, is attached to the body of the guitar. Raised ridges, called **frets**, are spaced along the finger board. **Strings** of nylon or steel are stretched across the sound hole from the **bridge** up to the **tuning pegs** at the end of the finger board. This instrument can be played by pressing the strings against the frets with one hand while strumming the guitar with the other. Instruments similar to the guitar are the banjo, the mandolin, the ukulele, and the violin.

Identify the parts of the guitar as labeled in the illustration. Match each letter with the name of a part.

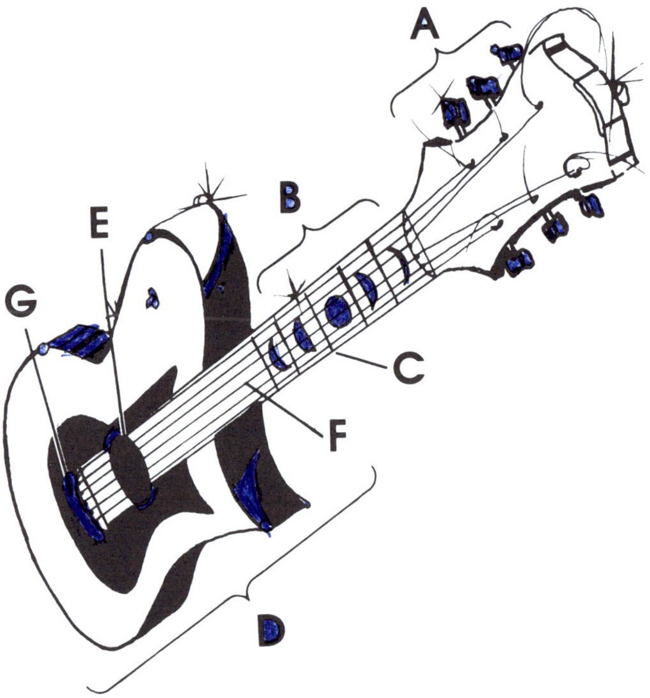

GUITAR PARTS

1. ______ body
2. ______ sound hole
3. ______ finger board
4. ______ frets
5. ______ strings
6. ______ bridge
7. ______ tuning pegs

The first sentence of the model introduces and describes the object that is defined in the paragraph.

8. What object is introduced? ______________________________

9. How is it described? ______________________________

Other sentences in the paragraph add to the definition by referring to specific characteristics of the subject. Next to each characteristic listed below, write those words from the model which help to define the guitar. Not all characteristics are referred to in the definition.

10. action ______________________________

11. color ______________________________

12. function ______________________________

13. materials ______________________________

14. parts ______________________________

15. shape ______________________________

16. size ______________________________

17. texture ______________________________

18. weight ______________________________

19. The concluding sentence compares the guitar to other instruments. List them here.

    ____

Score the Practice exercise using the Answer Key, and go on to the Composition part of this guide.

Composition

This part of the guide will help you to apply what you have learned about writing a paragraph using definition. Choose **one** topic and list as many characteristics of the subject as you can find. Use this list as you follow the plan for writing a paragraph using definition.

You may find it helpful to use reference sources such as the dictionary, encyclopedia, or other books. When you use information from reference sources, do not copy directly from the book. Always use your own words to rephrase what you have read.

Topics

An airplane

A telephone

An umbrella

A shark

The human heart

Plan

- In the first sentence, introduce and describe the subject that will be defined in your paragraph.
- Write at least **five** sentences in which you define your subject as completely as possible. Use this list of characteristics as a reference: action, color, function, materials, parts, shape, size, texture, weight.
- Write a concluding sentence for your paragraph.

Use the Checklist to help you review and revise your writing. Do this for all drafts and your final copy.

Checklist	**Yes**	**No**
1. Before I began my paragraph, I listed characteristics of the subject.	____	____
2. In the first sentence, I introduced and described the subject that is defined in the paragraph.	____	____
3. I defined my subject in sentences which refer to specific characteristics. (Check [✓] those that apply): action ____ color ____ function ____ materials ____ parts ____ shape ____ size ____ texture ____ weight ____	____	____
4. I wrote at least five sentences of definition.	____	____
5. I wrote a conclusion for my paragraph.	____	____
6. I used my own words to rephrase what I read.	____	____
7. I used transitions to connect ideas and create unity in my writing.	____	____
8. I wrote complete sentences that begin with capital letters, and used proper end punctuation.	____	____
9. I proofread and edited my composition, and wrote a corrected copy of my work.	____	____

Submit the completed writing assignment and Practice exercise to your instructor for evaluation.

18.

Using Definition: B

The first part of this guide gives you an opportunity to practice your grammar, usage, and punctuation. It can also be used to improve your spelling, learn new words, and sharpen your reading comprehension skills. These activities will help to improve your writing.

Skills Practice

Choose one or more of the following exercises and answer at least **thirty** questions:

A **corrective** exercise recommended by your instructor.

A **spelling** exercise from available materials.

A **vocabulary** exercise from available materials.

A **reading comprehension** exercise from available materials.

Record the number of questions you complete, and score the exercise using available answer keys. Then go on to the Composition part of this guide.

Composition

This section of the guide provides additional practice in writing a paragraph using definition. Choose an object to define and list as many characteristics of this object as you can find. Use this list as you follow the plan for writing a paragraph using definition. You may find it helpful to use reference sources such as the dictionary, encyclopedia, or other books. If you use reference sources, do not copy directly from the book. Use your own words to rephrase what you read.

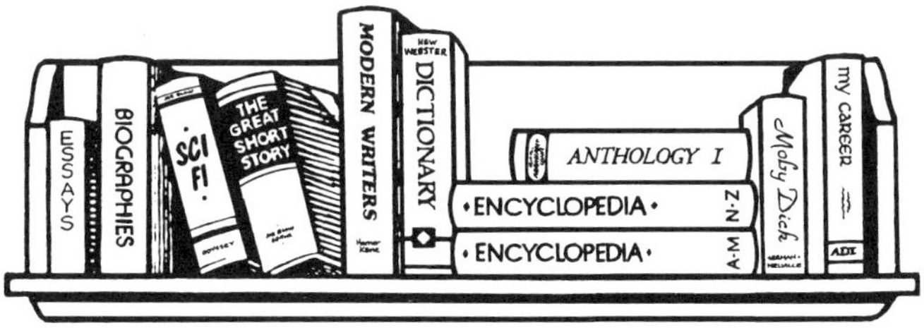

Plan

- In the first sentence, introduce and describe the subject that will be defined in your paragraph.
- Write at least **five** sentences in which you define your subject as completely as possible. Use this list of characteristics as a reference: action, color, function, materials, parts, shape, size, texture, weight.
- Write a concluding sentence for your paragraph.

Use the Checklist to help you review and revise your writing. Do this for all drafts and your final copy.

Checklist	**Yes**	**No**
1. Before I began my paragraph, I listed characteristics of the subject.	____	____
2. In the first sentence, I introduced and described the subject that is defined in the paragraph.	____	____
3. I defined my subject in sentences which refer to specific characteristics. (Check [✓] those that apply):	____	____
action ____ color ____ function ____ materials ____ parts ____ shape ____ size ____ texture ____ weight ____		
4. I wrote at least five sentences of definition.	____	____
5. I wrote a conclusion for my paragraph.	____	____
6. I used my own words to rephrase what I read.	____	____
7. I used transitions to connect ideas and create unity in my writing.	____	____
8. I wrote complete sentences that begin with capital letters, and used proper end punctuation.	____	____
9. I proofread and edited my composition, and I wrote a corrected copy of my work.	____	____

Submit the completed writing assignment and Practice exercise to your instructor for evaluation.

19.

Comparison and Contrast: A

This guide will help you to write a paragraph using comparison and contrast. **We use comparison and contrast to explain how things are alike and how they are different**. The subjects you write about must have at least one category in common. You can compare dogs with cats because both belong to the same category, *household pets.* You can compare dogs with elephants because both belong to the same category, *animals.* When you keep the category in mind, you have a focus for your writing.

- When you **compare** one subject to another, you show how the two are alike, or similar. **The dog, like the cat, is a household pet**.

- When you **contrast** two subjects, you show how they are different. **The dog, unlike the cat, is very dependent on its master**.

- Sometimes, both **comparison and contrast** are used in the same sentence. **Both the dog and the cat make good household pets, but a dog requires more attention than a cat.**

Key Words

To write a comparison and contrast paragraph, you will need to use transitional words and phrases that express opposite points of view. You will also be using transitions that show relationships between ideas. We have grouped these key words in two categories below.

Key words commonly used to express **comparison** include:

like	similar	as
same	in the same way	too
both	most important	have in common
the same as	similarly	as well as

Key words commonly used to express **contrast** include:

although	yet	whereas
however	but	while
differ	instead	unless
unlike	on the contrary	contrary to
even though	on the other hand	the reverse

Practice

Read each part of the following exercise and answer all **28** questions. In the model paragraph below, the author explains two subjects by using comparison and contrast.

> Apples and oranges are similar in some ways, yet they are also different. They are both fruits that grow on trees. Apples, however, do well in colder climates, while oranges grow best where it's hot year-round. The two fruits are both round and small, but their skins differ in thickness and in color. The orange is thick-skinned and orange in color, whereas the thin-skinned apple can be red, green, or yellow. You can eat the skin of an apple; however, the skin of an orange is inedible. The insides of both are juicy and delicious to eat. Most important, apples and oranges are very nutritious foods that satisfy your "sweet tooth."

Answer the questions below by filling in the blanks. Refer to the model to help you complete this exercise.

1. What two subjects are being compared in this paragraph?

   ______________________ and ______________________

2. To what general category do both of these subjects belong?

   ____

3. How many of the key words used in writing comparison and contrast can you find in the paragraph? ________________

4. List **five** of the key words. ____________________________

Listed below are characteristics of fruit that can be used in comparing and contrasting apples and oranges. Use the model to complete the chart below. Not every characteristic is referred to in the paragraph, so you will have some blanks. The first one is done for you.

CHARACTERISTIC	APPLES	ORANGES
where they grow	**trees**	**trees**
5. calories		
6. shape		
7. skin color(s)		
8. growing climate		
9. taste		
10. size		
11. skin (thick, thin)		
12. cost		
13. skin (edible, inedible)		
14. food value		
15. seeds		

For each of the following, indicate whether the sentence uses **comparison**, **contrast**, or **both**.

16. The banjo is very much like the guitar in its construction.

____

17. Day is light while dark is night.

____

18. Flowers and weeds are both plants, but people prefer flowers because of their beauty.

____

19. Lions, like tigers, are big cats that roam the jungle.

____

20. Although the dog is said to be man's best friend, cats are easier to care for.

____

21. Silver is less expensive than gold.

____

22. Although they have no arms, snakes can still climb as well as monkeys.

____

23. It's hot in the summer, but cold in the winter.

____

24. Both the sun and the moon are round.

____

25. The Civil War between the North and the South was, in some ways, similar to earlier wars.

____

26. Milk and soda are both beverages, but milk is a healthier drink.

____

27. Frank and John are the same height and weight, but John is much stronger.

____

28. Skiing, like ice skating, requires strong leg muscles and and a good sense of balance.

____

Score the Practice exercise using the Answer Key, and go on to the Composition part of this guide.

Composition

This part of the guide will help you apply what you have learned about writing a paragraph using comparison and contrast. Choose **one** topic and make a chart that compares and contrasts at least five characteristics of your subject. Use this list as you follow the plan for writing a paragraph using comparison and contrast.

Topics

Summer and winter

Youth and old age

Two sports of your choice

Men and women

Two of your friends

Plan

- Introduce the two subjects you will compare and contrast, and the category they have in common.
- Compare and contrast at least **five** characteristics of your subjects.
- Use the list of key words provided in the Practice exercise to help connect your ideas.
- Conclude your paragraph by telling the reader what you believe is the most important way in which your subjects are alike, or different.

Use the Checklist to help you review and revise your writing. Do this for all drafts and your final copy.

Checklist	**Yes**	**No**
1. Before I began my paragraph, I made a chart that compares and contrasts five characteristics of my subjects.	____	____
2. I began my paragraph by introducing the two subjects and the category they have in common.	____	____
3. I wrote sentences that compare and contrast at least five characteristics of my subjects.	____	____
4. I used key words associated with comparison and contrast to help connect ideas. These words are: ______________________	____	____
5. In my conclusion, I tell the reader the most important way in which my subjects are alike, or different.	____	____
6. I wrote complete sentences that begin with capital letters, and used proper end punctuation.	____	____
7. I proofread and edited my composition.	____	____
8. I wrote a corrected copy of my work.	____	____

Submit the completed writing assignment and Practice exercise to your instructor for evaluation.

20.

Comparison and Contrast: B

The first part of this guide gives you an opportunity to practice your grammar, usage, and punctuation. It can also be used to improve your spelling, learn new words, and sharpen your reading comprehension skills. These activities will help to improve your writing.

Skills Practice

Choose one or more of the following exercises and answer at least **thirty** questions:

A **corrective** exercise recommended by your instructor.

A **spelling** exercise from available materials.

A **vocabulary** exercise from available materials.

A **reading comprehension** exercise from available materials.

Record the number of questions you complete, and score the exercise using available answer keys. Then go on to the Composition part of this guide.

Composition

This section of the guide provides additional practice in writing a paragraph using comparison and contrast. Read a fiction or nonfiction selection from available book titles. You may need to read more than one selection to choose subjects. Select two people, places, things, or ideas from the reading to compare and contrast. Make a chart that compares and contrasts at least five characteristics of your two subjects. Use this chart as you follow the plan for writing a paragraph using comparison and contrast.

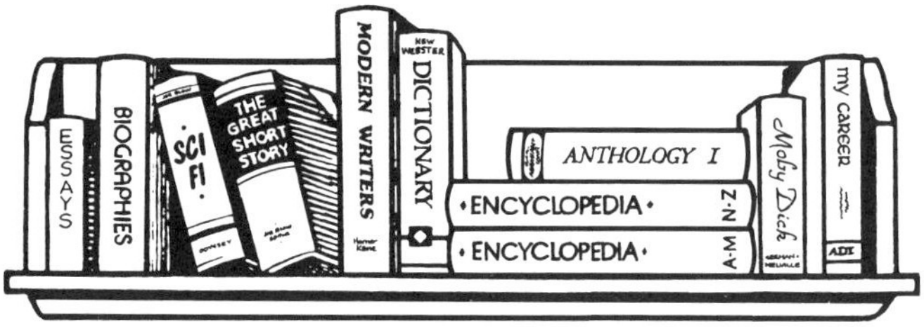

Plan

- Introduce the two subjects that you will compare and contrast, and the category they have in common.
- Compare and contrast at least **five** characteristics of your subjects.
- Use the list of key words provided in the Practice exercise to help connect your ideas.
- Conclude your paragraph by telling the reader what you believe is the most important way in which your subjects are alike, or different.

Use the Checklist to help you review and revise your writing. Do this for all drafts and your final copy.

Checklist	**Yes**	**No**
1. Before I began my paragraph, I made a chart that compares and contrasts five characteristics of my subjects.	____	____
2. I began my paragraph by introducing the two subjects and the category they have in common.	____	____
3. I wrote sentences that compare and contrast at least five characteristics of my subjects.	____	____
4. I used key words associated with comparison and contrast to help connect ideas. These words are: ________________________	____	____
5. In my conclusion, I tell the reader the most important way in which my subjects are alike, or different.	____	____
6. I wrote complete sentences that begin with capital letters, and used proper end punctuation.	____	____
7. I proofread and edited my composition.	____	____
8. I wrote a corrected copy of my work.	____	____

Submit the completed writing assignment and Practice exercise to your instructor for evaluation.

21.

Cause and Effect: A

This guide will help you to write a paragraph using cause and effect. Cause and effect are used to explain why something is the way it is. **The cause is the reason why, and the effect is the result.**

CAUSE
The boy stepped on a banana peel.

EFFECT
The boy fell.

The cause leads to the effect:

The boy stepped on a banana peel and **he fell.**

(cause) ⟶ (effect)

The effect is a result of the cause:

The boy fell because **he stepped on a banana peel.**

(effect) ⟵ (cause)

These are two different ways of saying the same thing about a cause and effect relationship.

Key Words

To write a cause and effect paragraph, you will need to use transitional words and phrases that help you restate main ideas. You will also be using transitions that show relationships between ideas. These key words are listed below.

if	thus	then	consequently
so	since	when	caused by
so that	because	due to	bring about
lead to	therefore	as a result	for this reason

Practice

Read each part of the following exercise and answer all **13** questions. In the model paragraph, the author uses cause and effect to explain how the custom of shaking hands came about.

> The custom of shaking hands developed as a result of fear and mistrust. At one time, men never went anywhere without a weapon because there was always the possibility of an attack. When strangers met, they made a point of moving their weapons aside and showing empty hands. Two men would join right hands in a firm clasp so that neither could reach for a dagger. If a man intended harm, he would never shake hands. Today, the clasping of hands is a way of introducing ourselves to others and saying that we are friend, not foe.

1. How many of the key words used to show cause and effect can you locate in the paragraph? ______________________

2. List the words. ______________________

Below are some statements based on the ideas presented in the model paragraph. Copy the sentences and write the word *cause* or *effect* in the parentheses that follow each phrase.

3. The custom of shaking hands (   ) developed because of fear and mistrust (   ).

4. Since most people carried weapons (   ), strangers signaled one another that they were friendly (   ).

5. Attack was always possible (   ); consequently, men brushed aside their weapons and showed empty hands (   ).

6. Men clasped their right hands (   ) so that neither could grasp a dagger (   ).

7. Suspicion (   ) led to the custom of shaking hands (   ).

The proverb below is a very old saying that uses cause and effect to tell the reader that even small details can be very important.

> For want of a nail the shoe was lost,
> For want of a shoe the horse was lost,
> For want of a horse the rider was lost,
> For want of a rider the battle was lost,
> For want of a battle the kingdom was lost,
> And all for the want of a horseshoe nail.

Copy the sentences below, and write the word *cause* or *effect* in the parentheses that follow each phrase. "For want of a nail" means the same thing as "because a nail was needed."

8. For want of a nail (   ) the shoe was lost (   ).

9. The horse was lost (   ) for want of a shoe (   ).

10. The rider was lost (   ) for want of a horse (   ).

11. For want of a rider (   ) the battle was lost (   ).

12. The kingdom was lost (   ) for want of a battle (   ).

13. All was lost (   ) for the want of a horseshoe nail (   ).

Score the Practice exercise using the Answer Key, and go on to the Composition part of this guide.

Composition

This part of the guide will help you apply what you have learned about writing a paragraph using cause and effect. Choose **one** topic and list five sets of causes and effects (how one thing leads to another). Use this list as you follow the plan for writing a paragraph using cause and effect.

You may find it helpful to use reference sources such as the dictionary, encyclopedia, or other books. When you use information from reference sources, do not copy directly from the book. Always use your own words to rephrase what you have read.

Topics

If I had three wishes

Laughter is good for you

Writing clearly is important

Major causes of the American Revolution

The law of gravity: what goes up must come down

Plan

- Introduce your subject in the first sentence of the paragraph.
- Write about your subject using cause and effect. Write at least **five** sentences for this part.
- Use the list of key words presented in the Practice exercise to help you connect ideas.
- Write a conclusion for your paragraph that summarizes the topic for the reader.

Use the Checklist to help you review and revise your writing. Do this for all drafts and your final copy.

Checklist	**Yes**	**No**
1. I listed sets of causes and effects about my topic. I began my paragraph by introducing the subject.	____	____
2. I wrote about my subject using cause and effect. I wrote at least five sentences for this part.	____	____
3. I used key words associated with cause and effect to help me connect ideas. These words are: ______________________	____	____
4. I wrote a conclusion that summarizes my topic for the reader.	____	____
5. I used my own words to rephrase what I read.	____	____
6. I wrote complete sentences that begin with capital letters, and used proper end punctuation.	____	____
7. I proofread and edited my composition.	____	____
8. I wrote a corrected copy of my work.	____	____

Submit the completed writing assignment and Practice exercise to your instructor for evaluation.

22.

Cause and Effect: B

The first part of this guide gives you an opportunity to practice your grammar, usage, and punctuation. It can also be used to improve your spelling, learn new words, and sharpen your reading comprehension skills. These activities will help to improve your writing.

Skills Practice

Choose one or more of the following exercises and answer at least **thirty** questions:

A **corrective** exercise recommended by your instructor.

A **spelling** exercise from available materials.

A **vocabulary** exercise from available materials.

A **reading comprehension** exercise from available materials.

Record the number of questions you complete, and score the exercise using available answer keys. Then go on to the Composition part of this guide.

Composition

This section of the guide provides additional practice in writing a paragraph using cause and effect. Read a fiction or a nonfiction selection from available book titles. Choose a topic that shows how one thing leads to another. List five sets of causes and effects. Use this list as you follow the plan for writing a paragraph using cause and effect. If you use reference sources, do not copy directly from the book. Use your own words to rephrase what you have read.

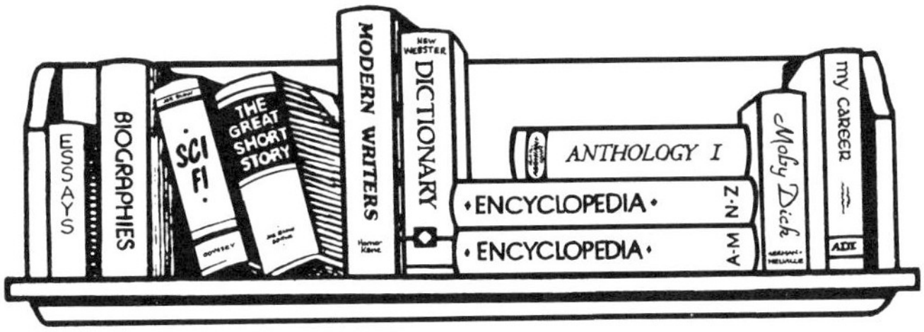

Plan

- Introduce your subject in the first sentence of the paragraph.
- Write about your subject using cause and effect. Write at least **five** sentences for this part.
- Use the list of key words presented in the Practice exercise to help you connect ideas.
- Write a conclusion for your paragraph that summarizes the topic for the reader.

Use the Checklist to help you review and revise your writing. Do this for all drafts and your final copy.

Checklist	**Yes**	**No**
1. I listed sets of causes and effects about my topic. I began my paragraph by introducing the subject.	_____	_____
2. I wrote about my subject using cause and effect. I wrote at least five sentences for this part.	_____	_____
3. I used key words associated with cause and effect to help me connect ideas. These words are: ______________________	_____	_____
4. I wrote a conclusion that summarizes my topic for the reader.	_____	_____
5. I used my own words to rephrase what I read.	_____	_____
6. I wrote complete sentences that begin with capital letters, and used proper end punctuation.	_____	_____
7. I proofread and edited my composition.	_____	_____
8. I wrote a corrected copy of my work.	_____	_____

Submit the completed writing assignment and Practice exercise to your instructor for evaluation.

23.

The Persuasive Paragraph: A

This guide will help you to write a persuasive paragraph. **Persuasive writing appeals to your ability to reason and to your emotions.** This approach attempts to make the reader think, feel, and even act in a certain way. Persuasion is usually successful when the writer provides good reasons for doing, or not doing, something. Writing persuasively will convince the reader to see things **your** way.

Practice

Read each part of the following exercise and answer all **23** questions. In the model persuasive paragraph, the author attempts to convince the reader to stop smoking. He does this by relating his own experience with smoking and giving specific reasons why he quit.

> If you smoke cigarettes and want to stop, you can. I smoked for more than twenty years before I quit. I puffed in the face of danger, even though I was aware that smoking is linked to lung cancer, heart disease, and other potentially fatal diseases. Why worry about the future? The reason I did eventually quit was because I realized that the quality of my life was declining. I didn't enjoy eating because I couldn't taste my food. My social contacts, both personal and business, were negatively affected by the smoke I blew in other people's faces. Smoking also cut my energy level considerably. I had trouble exercising, playing sports, and even walking up stairs. Is this beginning to sound familiar? I finally quit smoking so that I could enjoy the rest of my life. You can do the same for yourself!

In the model, the author introduces the topic with a statement that challenges the reader to do something, in this case give up smoking. "If you smoke cigarettes and want to stop, you can." This strong opening sentence gets the reader's attention. The author then supports his argument throughout the paragraph by offering very specific reasons for giving up smoking and by stating his opinions.

1. The author reinforces his argument by pointing to the connection between cigarettes and disease. Write that sentence here:
   Smoking is linked to lung cancer

2. The author further supports his argument with a firsthand account of how smoking affected his life. In how many ways was the quality of the author's life declining? 6

3. List each of the ways. eating, social contacts exercising, playing sports, walking up stairs

By addressing you directly, the author invites you to share his attitude toward the subject. Write the three sentences in which the author addresses the reader directly.

4. If you smoke cigarettes
5. Why worry about the future?
6. You can do the same for yourself.

In his conclusion, the author restates what he did, and why he did it. He then invites the reader to do the same. Write these two sentences.

7. I finally quit smoking so that I could enjoy the rest of my life.
8. You can do the same for yourself.

Sentences based on ideas presented in the model are listed below. Some offer facts which appeal to reason. Other sentences offer opinions that appeal to the emotions of the reader. Write the word *fact* in the blank after each sentence that appeals to reason. Write the word *opinion* in the blank after each sentence that appeals to emotion.

9. I smoked for twenty years before I quit. fact

10. I wanted to enjoy my life. opinion.

11. Smoking is linked to lung cancer. fact

12. If you want to stop smoking, you can! ____________

13. I puffed in the face of danger. ____________

14. I had trouble exercising, playing sports, and climbing stairs.

____

15. Is this beginning to sound familiar to you? opinion

16. Why worry about the future? opinion

17. I couldn't taste my food. ____________

18. People told me they didn't like smoke blown in their faces.

____

19. I didn't enjoy eating. ____________

20. Smoking cut my energy level considerably. ____________

21. I felt the quality of my life was declining. opinion

22. I finally stopped smoking cigarettes. ____________

23. You can do the same for yourself. ____________

Score the Practice exercise using the Answer Key, and go on to the Composition part of this guide.

Composition

This part of the guide will help you apply what you have learned about writing a persuasive paragraph. Choose **one** topic and make a list of facts and another of opinions about the issue you have selected. You can argue for or against this issue. Use your lists as you follow the plan for writing a persuasive paragraph in which you try to convince the reader to accept your point of view.

Topics

Gossip is harmless.

The drinking age should be twenty-one.

Violence on television is harmful to children.

Smoking in public places should be prohibited.

Every citizen should exercise his or her right to vote.

Plan

- In your first sentence, make a strong statement or ask a question that gets the reader's attention.
- Write at least **five** sentences in which you offer facts and opinions that support your argument.
- Conclude the paragraph by suggesting an outcome for the reader to consider which further supports your argument.

Use the Checklist to help you review and revise your writing. Do this for all drafts and your final copy.

Checklist	**Yes**	**No**
1. I made one list of facts and another of opinions about my subject.	____	____
2. The first sentence of my paragraph is a strong statement, or question, that gets the reader's attention.	____	____
3. I wrote at least five sentences in which I offer facts and opinions that support my argument.	____	____
4. I concluded my paragraph by suggesting an outcome for the reader to consider which further supports my argument.	____	____
5. I used transitions to connect ideas and create unity in my writing.	____	____
6. I wrote complete sentences that begin with capital letters, and used proper end punctuation.	____	____
7. I proofread and edited my composition.	____	____
8. I wrote a corrected copy of my work.	____	____

Submit the completed writing assignment and Practice exercise to your instructor for evaluation.

24.

The Persuasive Paragraph: B

The first part of this guide gives you an opportunity to practice your grammar, usage, and punctuation. It can also be used to improve your spelling, learn new words, and sharpen your reading comprehension skills. These activities will help to improve your writing.

Skills Practice

Choose one or more of the following exercises and answer at least **thirty** questions:

A **corrective** exercise recommended by your instructor.

A **spelling** exercise from available materials.

A **vocabulary** exercise from available materials.

A **reading comprehension** exercise from available materials.

Record the number of questions you complete, and score the exercise using available answer keys. Then go on to the Composition part of this guide.

Composition

This section of the guide provides additional practice in writing a persuasive paragraph. Read a fiction or nonfiction selection from available book titles. Choose an issue from the reading about which you have strong feelings. Make a list of facts and another of opinions about the subject you have selected. Use these lists as you follow the plan for writing a persuasive paragraph in which you try to convince the reader to accept your point of view.

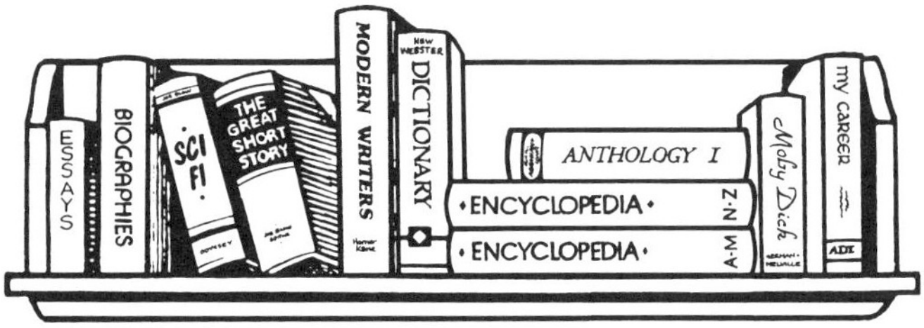

Plan

- In your first sentence, make a strong statement or ask a question that gets the reader's attention.
- Write at least **five** sentences in which you offer facts and opinions that support your argument.
- Conclude the paragraph by suggesting an outcome for the reader to consider which further supports your argument.

Use the Checklist to help you review and revise your writing. Do this for all drafts and your final copy.

Checklist	**Yes**	**No**
1. I made one list of facts and another of opinions about my subject.	____	____
2. The first sentence of my paragraph is a strong statement, or question, that gets the reader's attention.	____	____
3. I wrote at least five sentences in which I offer facts and opinions that support my argument.	____	____
4. I concluded my paragraph by suggesting an outcome for the reader to consider which further supports my argument.	____	____
5. I used transitions to connect ideas and create unity in my writing.	____	____
6. I wrote complete sentences that begin with capital letters, and used proper end punctuation.	____	____
7. I proofread and edited my composition.	____	____
8. I wrote a corrected copy of my work.	____	____

Submit the completed writing assignment and Practice exercise to your instructor for evaluation.

25.

The Three Paragraph Essay: A

This guide will help you to write a three paragraph essay. Both the single paragraph and the three paragraph essay have an **introduction**, a **middle**, and a **conclusion**. The difference is that the three paragraph essay allows for more detailed development of each of these sections.

In the three paragraph essay:

- the first paragraph introduces the topic of the essay and indicates a plan for its development.
- the middle paragraph develops the topic by providing supporting details: facts, examples, and descriptions.
- the concluding paragraph restates the topic and summarizes the main points of the essay.

Practice

Read each part of the following exercise and answer all **9** questions. In the model essay, the author combines exposition (explanation) with persuasion to make recommendations about caring for yourself when you have a cold.

Have you ever tried to wish away a cold? The common cold, with its accompanying cough, fever, aches and pains, can be effectively treated by you. If you follow the advice presented here, you can minimize the discomforts of a cold.

There are three basic steps to follow in curing the common cold. Bundle up in bed and get lots of rest. The body heals itself while in a state of rest and relaxation. Use a vaporizer during the night so that you will inhale steam while you sleep. Above all, drink plenty of liquids. Fresh squeezed lemon juice mixed with honey and hot water works wonders. Drink about ten to twelve glasses of liquids daily, preferably fruit juices, herb teas and water. Sleep, moist air to breathe, and liquids to drink will help to make you well again.

Take time to care for yourself when you have a cold. You will be rewarded by feeling healthier, sooner. You may not be able to wish away a cold, but you can make yourself feel a lot better.

Use the model essay to answer the questions below.

The Introductory Paragraph

Write the sentence that asks a question which appeals to the reader's interest.

1. ____

Write the sentence that introduces the topic of the essay.

2. ____

Write the sentence that states a plan for the development of the essay.

3. ____

The Development Paragraph

Write a sentence that clearly states the topic to be developed in **this** paragraph.

4. ____

How many sentences contain supporting details: facts, examples, and descriptions that relate to the topic of **this** paragraph?

5. ____

Write the sentence which summarizes the information presented in **this** section of the essay.

6. ____

The Concluding Paragraph

Write the sentence that restates the topic of the essay.

7. ____

Write the sentence that supports the restatement.

8. ____

Write the sentence which sums up the author's opinion and concludes the essay.

9. ____

Score the Practice exercise using the Answer Key, and go on to the Composition part of this guide.

Composition

This part of the guide will help you apply what you have learned about writing a three paragraph essay. Write your essay about **one** of the topics listed below. Apply what you have learned from previous guides. Follow the outline to write your composition.

Topics

A decision that changed my life (**narrative**)

An exciting sports event (**descriptive**)

My favorite hobby (**expository**)

Why read the newspaper? (**persuasive**)

Travel: where I would go, what I would do (**expository**)

Outline

I. The Introductory Paragraph

   A. Begin with a strong statement, or question, that appeals to the reader's interest.

   B. Make a general statement that introduces your topic.

   C. State a plan of development for this essay.

II. The Development Paragraph

   A. First, state what will be discussed in this paragraph.

   B. Offer specifics: facts, details, information, evidence, and opinions pertaining to the topic of this paragraph.

   C. Briefly summarize the major point of this paragraph.

III. The Concluding Paragraph

   A. Restate the topic of the essay.

   B. Support the restatement in a sentence or two.

   C. Express your opinion and conclude the essay.

Use the Checklist to help you review and revise your writing. Do this for all drafts and your final copy.

Checklist	**Yes**	**No**
1. In my introductory paragraph I appeal to the reader's interest, state the topic of the essay, and present a plan for development.	____	____
2. In my development paragraph I state the topic for this paragraph, offer specifics, and summarize what is presented here.	____	____
3. In my concluding paragraph I restate the topic of the essay, support it, express my opinion, and conclude the essay.	____	____
4. I used transitions to connect ideas and create unity in my writing.	____	____
5. I wrote complete sentences that begin with capital letters, and used proper end punctuation.	____	____
6. I proofread and edited my composition.	____	____
7. I wrote a corrected copy of my work.	____	____

Submit the completed writing assignment and Practice exercise to your instructor for evaluation.

26.

The Three Paragraph Essay: B

The first part of this guide gives you an opportunity to practice your grammar, usage, and punctuation. It can also be used to improve your spelling, learn new words, and sharpen your reading comprehension skills. These activities will help to improve your writing.

Skills Practice

Choose one or more of the following exercises and answer at least **thirty** questions:

A **corrective** exercise recommended by your instructor.

A **spelling** exercise from available materials.

A **vocabulary** exercise from available materials.

A **reading comprehension** exercise from available materials.

Record the number of questions you complete, and score the exercise using available answer keys. Then go on to the Composition part of this guide.

Composition

This section of the guide provides additional practice in writing a three paragraph essay. Choose a nonfiction selection to read from available book titles. Write a three paragraph essay in which you explain the important points the author makes with reference to the topic. Follow the outline to write your essay.

Outline

I. The Introductory Paragraph

A. Begin with a strong statement, or question, that appeals to the reader's interest.

B. Make a general statement that introduces your topic.

C. State a plan of development for the essay.

II. The Development Paragraph

A. First, state what will be discussed in this paragraph.

B. Offer specifics: facts, details, information, evidence, and opinions pertaining to the topic of this paragraph.

C. Briefly summarize the major point of this paragraph.

III. The Concluding Paragraph

A. Restate the topic of the essay.

B. Support the restatement in a sentence or two.

C. Express your opinion and conclude the essay.

Use the Checklist to help you review and revise your writing. Do this for all drafts and your final copy.

Checklist	**Yes**	**No**
1. In my introductory paragraph I appeal to the reader's interest, state the topic of the essay, and present a plan for development.	____	____
2. In my development paragraph I state the topic for this paragraph, offer specifics, and summarize what is presented here.	____	____
3. In my concluding paragraph I restate the topic of the essay, support it, express my opinion, and conclude the essay.	____	____
4. I used transitions to connect ideas and create unity in my writing.	____	____
5. I wrote complete sentences that begin with capital letters, and used proper end punctuation.	____	____
6. I proofread and edited my composition.	____	____
7. I wrote a corrected copy of my work.	____	____

Submit the completed writing assignment and Practice exercise to your instructor for evaluation.

III.

About Fiction

Fiction is imaginative literature which includes such forms as: the short story, the novel, poetry, and drama. This section focuses on the short story. You will have an opportunity to analyze the short story and create one of your own.

The novel is very much like the short story. Both share the same elements, but the novel is longer and more complex. The work that you do in writing about the short story will help you to understand how novels are written.

When you begin work in this section, check with your instructor about selecting a novel that you would like to read. Plan to complete the novel before you start The Book Report guide.

Guides

27.

The Short Story: A

This guide will help you to understand the short story. A **short story** tells about a single event or experience which illustrates some aspect of life. A short story creates an impression for the reader through **setting**, **characterization**, **conflict and plot**, **theme**, and **point of view**. All of these elements contribute to producing one dominant effect in the story.

Elements of the Short Story

Setting The setting tells the reader where and when the story takes place. It also sets forth the background information and creates atmosphere for the story.

Characterization Characterization is the creation of imaginary people who appear to be real to the reader.

Conflict and Plot A conflict is a problem in the story that needs to be resolved. A plot is a series of events through which the author reveals what is happening, to whom, and why. Twists and turns in the plot create complications and tension. The point of greatest tension in the story is called the climax.

Theme The theme of the story conveys the author's message about people and the world in which we live. The theme is expressed through all the elements of the short story.

Point of View Point of view refers to the position of the narrator of the story and what the narrator sees from that vantage point.

"The Boy Who Painted Christ Black" is a short story by John Henrik Clarke. Mr. Clarke is a distinguished American author and historian who is professor of Black and Puerto Rican studies at Hunter College, City University of New York. The story takes place when segregated schools were the rule. It was published in 1940, fourteen years before the Supreme Court decision, *Brown vs. The Board of Education of Topeka, Kansas,* signaled the end of legally segregated schools. Read the story, then complete the exercises that follow. Use the dictionary to look up the definition of unfamiliar words.

The Boy Who Painted Christ Black

John Henrik Clarke

He was the smartest boy in the Muscogee County School—for colored children. Everybody even remotely connected with the school knew this. The teacher always pronounced his name with profound gusto as she pointed him out as the ideal student. Once I heard her say: "If he were white he might, some day, become President." Only Aaron Crawford wasn't white; quite the contrary. His skin was so solid black that it glowed, reflecting an inner virtue that was strange, and beyond my comprehension.

In many ways he looked like something that was awkwardly put together. Both his nose and his lips seemed a trifle too large for his face. To say he was ugly would be unjust and to say he was handsome would be gross exaggeration. Truthfully, I could never make up my mind about him. Sometimes he looked like something out of a book of ancient history . . . looked as if he was left over from that magnificent era before the machine age came and marred the earth's natural beauty.

His great variety of talent often startled the teachers. This caused his classmates to look upon him with a mixed feeling of awe and envy.

Before Thanksgiving, he always drew turkeys and pumpkins on the blackboard. On George Washington's birthday, he drew large American flags surrounded by little hatchets. It was these small masterpieces that made him the most talked-about colored boy in Columbus, Georgia. The Negro principal of the Muscogee County School said he would some day be a great painter, like Henry O. Tanner.

For the teacher's birthday, which fell on a day about a week before commencement, Aaron Crawford painted the picture that caused an uproar, and a turning point, at the Muscogee County School. The moment he entered the room that morning, all eyes fell on him. Besides his torn book holder, he was carrying a large-framed concern wrapped in old newspapers. As he went to his seat, the teacher's eyes followed his every motion, a curious wonderment mirrored in them conflicting with the half-smile that wreathed her face.

Aaron put his books down, then smiling broadly, advanced toward the teacher's desk. His alert eyes were so bright with joy that they were almost frightening. The children were leaning forward in their seats, staring greedily at him; a restless anticipation was rampant within every breast.

Already the teacher sensed that Aaron had a present for her. Still smiling, he placed it on her desk and began to help her unwrap it. As the last piece of paper fell from the large frame, the teacher jerked her hand away from it suddenly, her eyes flickering unbelievingly. Amidst the rigid tension, her heavy breathing was distinct and frightening. Temporarily, there was no other sound in the room.

Aaron stared questioningly at her and she moved her hand back to the present cautiously, as if it were a living thing with vicious characteristics. I am sure it was the one thing she least expected.

With a quick, involuntary movement I rose up from my desk. A series of submerged murmurs spread through the room, rising to a distinct monotone. The teacher turned toward the children, staring reproachfully. They did not move their eyes from the present that Aaron had brought her. . . . It was a large picture of Christ—painted black!

Aaron Crawford went back to his seat, a feeling of triumph reflecting in his every movement.

The teacher faced us. Her curious half-smile had blurred into a mild bewilderment. She searched the bright faces before her and started to smile again, occasionally stealing quick glances at the large picture propped on her desk, as though doing so were forbidden amusement.

"Aaron," she spoke at last, a slight tinge of uncertainty in her tone, "this is a most welcome present. Thanks. I will treasure it." She paused, then went on speaking, a trifle more coherent than before. "Looks like you are going to be quite an artist. . . . Suppose you come forward and tell the class how you came to paint this remarkable picture."

When he rose to speak, to explain about the picture, a hush fell tightly over the room, and the children gave him all of their attention . . . something they rarely did for the teacher. He did not speak at first; he just stood there in front of the room, toying absently with his hands, observing his audience carefully, like a great concert artist.

"It was like this," he said, placing full emphasis on every word. "You see, my uncle who lives in New York teaches classes in Negro history at the Y.M.C.A. When he visited us last year he was telling me about the many black folks who have made history. He said black folks were once the most powerful people on earth. When I asked him about Christ, he said no one ever proved whether he was black or white. Somehow a feeling came over me that he was a black man, 'cause he was so kind and forgiving, kinder than I have ever seen white people be. So, when I painted his picture I couldn't help but paint it as I thought it was."

After this, the little artist sat down, smiling broadly, as if he had gained entrance to a great storehouse of knowledge that ordinary people could neither acquire nor comprehend.

The teacher, knowing nothing else to do under prevailing circumstances, invited the children to rise from their seats and come forward so they could get a complete view of Aaron's unique piece of art.

When I came close to the picture, I noticed it was painted with the kind of paint you get in the five and ten cent stores. Its shape was blurred slightly, as if someone had jarred the frame before the paint had time to dry. The eyes of Christ were deep-set and sad, very much like those of Aaron's father, who was a deacon in the local Baptist Church. This picture of Christ looked much different from the one I saw hanging on the wall when I was in Sunday School. It looked more like a helpless Negro, pleading silently for mercy.

For the next few days, there was much talk about Aaron's picture.

The school term ended the following week and Aaron's picture, along with the best handwork done by the students that year, was on display in the assembly room. Naturally, Aaron's picture graced the place of honor.

There was no book work to be done on commencement day and joy was rampant among the children. The girls in their brightly colored dresses gave the school the delightful air of Spring awakening.

In the middle of the day all the children were gathered in the small assembly. On this day we were always favored with a visit from a man whom all the teachers spoke of with mixed esteem and fear. Professor Danual, they called him, and they always pronounced his name with reverence. He was supervisor of all the city schools, including those small and poorly equipped ones set aside for colored children. The great man arrived almost at the end of our commencement exercises. On seeing him enter the hall, the children rose, bowed courteously, and sat down again, their eyes examining him as if he were a circus freak.

He was a tall white man with solid gray hair that made his lean face seem paler than it actually was. His eyes were the clearest blue I have ever seen. They were the only life-like things about him.

As he made his way to the front of the room the Negro principal, George Du Vaul, was walking ahead of him, cautiously preventing anything from getting in his way. As he passed me, I heard the teachers, frightened, sucking in their breath, felt the tension tightening.

A large chair was in the center of the rostrum. It had been daintily polished and the janitor had laboriously recushioned its bottom. The supervisor went straight to it without being guided, knowing that this pretty splendor was reserved for him.

Presently the Negro principal introduced the distinguished guest and he favored us with a short speech. It wasn't a very important speech. Almost at the end of it, I remember him saying something about he wouldn't be surprised if one of us boys grew up to be a great colored man, like Booker T. Washington.

After he sat down, the school chorus sang two spirituals and the girls in the fourth grade did an Indian folk dance. This brought the commencement program to an end.

After this the supervisor came down from the rostrum, his eyes tinged with curiosity, and began to view the array of handwork on display in front of the chapel.

Suddenly his face underwent a strange rejuvenation. His clear blue eyes flickered in astonishment. He was looking at Aaron Crawford's picture of Christ. Mechanically he moved his stooped form closer to the picture and stood gazing fixedly at it, curious and undecided, as though it were a dangerous animal that would rise any moment and spread destruction.

We waited tensely for his next movement. The silence was almost suffocating. At last he twisted himself around and began to search the grim faces before him. The fiery glitter of his eyes abated slightly as they rested on the Negro principal, protestingly.

"Who painted this sacrilegious nonsense?" he demanded sharply.

"I painted it, sir." These were Aaron's words, spoken hesitantly.

He wetted his lips timidly and looked up at the supervisor, his eyes voicing a sad plea for understanding.

He spoke again, this time coherently. "Th' principal said a colored person have jes as much right paintin' Jesus black as a white person have paintin' him white. And he says. . . ." At this point he halted abruptly, as if to search for his next words. A strong tinge of bewilderment dimmed the glow of his solid black face. He stammered out a few more words, then stopped again.

The supervisor strode a few steps toward him. At last color had swelled some of the lifelessness out of his lean face.

"Well, go on!" he said, enragedly, ". . . I'm still listening."

Aaron moved his lips pathetically but no words passed them. His eyes wandered around the room, resting finally, with an air of hope, on the face of the Negro principal. After a moment, he jerked his face in another direction, regretfully, as if something he had said had betrayed an understanding between him and the principal.

Presently the principal stepped forward to defend the school's prize student.

"I encouraged the boy in painting that picture," he said firmly. "And it was with my permission that he brought the picture into this school. I don't think the boy is so far wrong in painting Christ black. The artists of all other races have painted whatsoever God they worship to resemble themselves. I see no reason why we should be immune from that privilege. After all, Christ was born in that part of the world that had always been predominantly populated by colored people. There is a strong possibility that he could have been a Negro."

But for the monotonous lull of heavy breathing, I would have sworn that his words had frozen everyone in the hall. I had never heard the little principal speak so boldly to anyone, black or white.

The supervisor swallowed dumbfoundedly. His face was aglow in silent rage.

"Have you been teaching these children things like that?" he asked the Negro principal, sternly.

"I have been teaching them that their race has produced great kings and queens as well as slaves and serfs," the principal said. "The time is long overdue when we should let the world know that we erected and enjoyed the benefits of a splendid civilization long before the people of Europe had a written language."

The supervisor coughed. His eyes bulged menacingly as he spoke. "You are not being paid to teach such things in this school, and I am demanding your resignation for overstepping your limit as principal."

George Du Vaul did not speak. A strong quiver swept over his sullen face. He revolved himself slowly and walked away out of the room toward the office.

The supervisor's eyes followed him until he was out of focus. Then he murmured under his breath: "There'll be a lot of fuss in this world if you start people thinking that Christ was a nigger."

Some of the teachers followed the principal out of the chapel, leaving the crestfallen children restless and in a quandary about what to do next. Finally we started back to our rooms. The supervisor was behind me. I heard him murmur to himself: "Damn, if niggers ain't getting smarter."

A few days later I heard that the principal had accepted a summer job as art instructor of a small high school somewhere in south Georgia and had gotten permission from Aaron's parents to take him along so he could continue to encourage him in his painting.

I was on my way home when I saw him leaving his office. He was carrying a large briefcase and some books tucked under his arm. He had already said good-bye to all the teachers. And strangely, he did not look brokenhearted. As he headed for the large front door, he readjusted his horn-rimmed glasses, but did not look back. An air of triumph gave more dignity to his soldierly stride. He had the appearance of a man who had done a great thing, something greater than any ordinary man would do.

Aaron Crawford was waiting outside for him. They walked down the street together. He put his arm around Aaron's shoulder affectionately. He was talking sincerely to Aaron about something, and Aaron was listening, deeply earnest.

I watched them until they were so far down the street that their forms had begun to blur. Even from this distance I could see they were still walking in brisk, dignified strides, like two people who had won some sort of victory.

Practice

Read each part of the following exercise and answer all **15** questions.

1. Write the title of the short story you have just read.

   ____

2. The author of this story is ________________________

3. The person telling the story is:
   a. Aaron.
   b. the principal.
   c. another student in the class.

4. The story takes place in:
   a. a segregated school in Columbus, Georgia.
   b. a segregated school in New York City.
   c. an integrated school in the South.

5. The story was published in:
   a. 1920 b. 1940 c. 1960

There are five characters in the story. Next to the name of each character, place the letter of the description that fits best.

Description

a. This person is a classmate of Aaron's.
b. This person defends Aaron against the criticism of the supervisor.
c. This person is a tall white man with gray hair.
d. This person is artistic and an ideal student.
e. This person receives a gift from Aaron.

Characters

6. ______ Aaron Crawford
7. ______ the teacher
8. ______ the principal
9. ______ the narrator
10. ______ the supervisor

For questions 11 through 15, choose the best answer: **a**, **b**, or **c**.

11. The story presents a struggle between:

    a. man and nature.
    b. man and society.
    c. man and the unknown.

12. A complication in the plot occurs when:

    a. the supervisor notices Aaron's painting during commencement.
    b. Aaron explains the painting to the class.
    c. the principal and Aaron leave together for a new school.

13. The point of greatest tension in the story occurs when:

    a. Aaron gives the teacher a painting for her birthday.
    b. the supervisor demands the principal's resignation.
    c. the principal steps forward to speak in defense of Aaron.

14. What happens to the principal at the end of the story?

    a. He apologizes to the supervisor and gets to keep his job.
    b. He scolds Aaron for mentioning his name to the supervisor.
    c. He resigns from his job and moves on to another school.

15. Which statement below best conveys the author's message?

    a. It is important to stand up for your beliefs.
    b. Young people should not question authority.
    c. Do as you're told, and you'll keep your job.

Score the Practice exercise using the Answer Key, and go on to the Composition part of this guide.

Composition

This part of the guide will help you apply what you have learned about the short story. Write a three paragraph essay about "The Boy Who Painted Christ Black." Follow the outline to write your essay.

Outline

I. The Introductory Paragraph

A. State the title and author of the story.
B. Tell where and when the story takes place.
C. Introduce the important (main) characters.
D. Indicate who narrates the story.
E. Describe the conflict (problem) in the story.

II. The Development Paragraph

A. How is the conflict introduced in the story?
B. What important events lead to further complications in the plot?
C. What is the point of greatest tension in this story?
D. How is the conflict resolved?

III. The Concluding Paragraph

A. How does the story end?
B. What is the author's message in this story?
C. How does the message, or theme, apply to people in general?
D. Tell why you did, or did not, like the story.

Use the Checklist to help you review and revise your writing. Do this for all drafts and your final copy.

Checklist	**Yes**	**No**
1. In my first paragraph I introduce the title and author of the story, the setting, the narrator, characters, and the conflict.	____	____
2. In my development paragraph I indicate how the conflict began, complications in the plot, the climax, and how the conflict is resolved.	____	____
3. In my concluding paragraph I tell how the story ends, what I believe the author is saying, and how I feel about the story.	____	____
4. I used transitions to connect ideas and create unity in my writing.	____	____
5. I proofread and edited my composition.	____	____
6. I wrote a corrected copy of my work.	____	____

Submit the completed writing assignment and Practice exercise to your instructor for evaluation.

28.

The Short Story: B

The first part of this guide gives you an opportunity to practice your grammar, usage, and punctuation. It can also be used to improve your spelling, learn new words, and sharpen your reading comprehension skills. These activities will help to improve your writing.

Skills Practice

Choose one or more of the following exercises and answer at least **thirty** questions:

A **corrective** exercise recommended by your instructor.

A **spelling** exercise from available materials.

A **vocabulary** exercise from available materials.

A **reading comprehension** exercise from available materials.

Record the number of questions you complete, and score the exercise using available answer keys. Then go on to the composition part of this guide.

Composition

This section of the guide provides additional practice in writing about the short story. Choose a story to read from available book titles. Write a three paragraph essay in which you analyze the short story. Follow the outline to write your essay.

Outline

I. The Introductory Paragraph

A. State the title and author of the story.
B. Tell where and when the story takes place.
C. Introduce the important (main) characters.
D. Indicate who narrates the story.
E. Describe the conflict (problem) in the story.

II. The Development Paragraph

A. How is the conflict introduced in the story?
B. What important events lead to further complications in the plot?
C. What is the point of greatest tension in this story?
D. How is the conflict resolved?

III. The Concluding Paragraph

A. How does the story end?
B. What is the author's message in this story?
C. How does the message, or theme, apply to people in general?
D. Tell why you did, or did not, like the story.

Use the Checklist to help you review and revise your writing. Do this for all drafts and your final copy.

Checklist	**Yes**	**No**
1. In my first paragraph I introduce the title and author of the story, the setting, the narrator, characters, and the conflict.	_____	_____
2. In my development paragraph I indicate how the conflict began, complications in the plot, the climax, and how the conflict is resolved.	_____	_____
3. In my concluding paragraph I tell how the story ends, what I believe the author is saying, and how I feel about the story.	_____	_____
4. I used transitions to connect ideas and create unity in my writing.	_____	_____
5. I proofread and edited my composition.	_____	_____
6. I wrote a corrected copy of my work.	_____	_____

Submit the completed writing assignment and Practice exercise to your instructor for evaluation.

29.

Characterization

This guide will help you to understand what characterization is and how it is used. **Characterization** is the creation of imaginary people who are so believable that the reader views them as real. The **character's name**, **physical appearance**, **actions**, **words**, **thoughts**, and **feelings** all contribute to creating this impression. What others say and how they feel about a character gives us additional insight into that character. This information is provided by the narrator of the story.

"All the Years of Her Life" is a short story by Morley Callaghan, a well-known Canadian novelist. The story is about a boy who often gets into trouble and is always rescued by his mother. The author focuses on three characters as a way of telling the story. Read the story, then complete the exercises that follow. Use the dictionary to look up the definition of unfamiliar words.

All the Years of Her Life

Morley Callaghan

They were closing the drugstore, and Alfred Higgins, who had just taken off his white jacket, was putting on his coat and getting ready to go home. The little gray-haired man, Sam Carr, who owned the drugstore, was bending down behind the cash register, and when Alfred Higgins passed him, he looked up and said softly, "Just a moment, Alfred. One moment before you go."

The soft, confident, quiet way in which Sam Carr spoke made Alfred start to button his coat nervously. He felt sure his face was white. Sam Carr usually said, "Good night," brusquely, without looking up. In the six months he had been working in the drugstore Alfred had never heard his employer speak softly like that. His heart began to beat so loud it was hard for him to get his breath. "What is it, Mr. Carr?" he asked.

"Maybe you'd be good enough to take a few things out of your pocket and leave them here before you go," Sam Carr said.

"What things? What are you talking about?"

"You've got a compact and a lipstick and at least two tubes of toothpaste in your pocket, Alfred."

"What do you mean? Do you think I'm crazy?" Alfred blustered. His face got red and he knew he looked fierce with indignation. But Sam Carr, standing by the door with his blue eyes shining bright behind his glasses and his lips moving underneath his gray mustache, only nodded his head a few times, and then Alfred grew very frightened and he didn't know what to say.

Slowly he raised his hand and dipped it into his pocket, and with his eyes never meeting Sam Carr's eyes, he took out a blue compact and two tubes of toothpaste and a lipstick, and he laid them one by one on the counter.

"Petty thieving, eh, Alfred?" Sam Carr said. "And maybe you'd be good enough to tell me how long this has been going on."

"This is the first time I ever took anything."

"So now you think you'll tell me a lie, eh? What kind of a sap do I look like, huh? I don't know what goes on in my own store, eh? I tell you you've been doing this pretty steady," Sam Carr said as he went over and stood behind the cash register.

Ever since Alfred had left school he had been getting in trouble wherever he worked. He lived at home with his mother and his father, who was a printer. His two older brothers were married and his sister had got married last year, and it would have been all right for his parents now if Alfred had only been able to keep a job.

While Sam Carr smiled and stroked the side of his face very delicately with the tips of his fingers, Alfred began to feel that familiar terror growing in him that had been in him every time he had got into such trouble.

"I liked you," Sam Carr was saying. "I liked you and would have trusted you, and now look what I got to do." While Alfred watched with his alert, frightened blue eyes, Sam Carr drummed with his fingers on the counter. "I don't like to call a cop in point-blank," he was saying as he looked very worried. "You're a fool, and maybe I should call your father and tell him you're a fool. Maybe I should let them know I'm going to have you locked up."

"My father's not at home. He's a printer. He works nights," Alfred said.

"Who's at home?"

"My mother, I guess."

"Then we'll see what she says." Sam Carr went to the phone and dialed the number. Alfred was not so much ashamed, but there was that deep fright growing in him, and he blurted out arrogantly, like a strong, full-grown man, "Just a minute. You don't need to draw anybody else in. You don't need to tell her." He wanted to sound like a swaggering, big guy who could look after himself, yet the old, childish hope was in him, the longing that someone at home would come and help him. "Yeah, that's right, he's in trouble," Mr. Carr was saying. "Yeah, your boy works for me. You'd better come down in a hurry." And when he was finished Mr. Carr went over to the door and looked out at the street and watched the people passing in the late summer night. "I'll keep my eye out for a cop," was all he said.

Alfred knew how his mother would come rushing in; she would rush in with her eyes blazing, or maybe she would be crying, and she would push him away when he tried to talk to her, and make him feel her dreadful contempt; yet he longed that she might come before Mr. Carr saw the cop on the beat passing the door.

While they waited—and it seemed a long time—they did not speak, and when at last they heard someone tapping on the closed door, Mr. Carr, turning the latch, said crisply, "Come in, Mrs. Higgins." He looked hard-faced and stern.

Mrs. Higgins must have been going to bed when he telephoned, for her hair was tucked in loosely under her hat, and her hand at her throat held her light coat tightly across her chest so her dress would not show. She came in, large and plump, with a little smile on her friendly face. Most of the store lights had been turned out and at first she did not see Alfred, who was standing in the shadow at the end of the counter. Yet as soon as she saw him she did not look as Alfred thought she would look: she smiled, her blue eyes never wavered, and with a calmness and dignity that made them forget that her clothes seemed to have been thrown on her, she put out her hand to Mr. Carr and said politely, "I'm Mrs. Higgins. I'm Alfred's mother."

Mr. Carr was a little embarrassed by her lack of terror and her simplicity, and he hardly knew what to say to her, so she asked, "Is Alfred in trouble?"

"He is. He's been taking things from the store. I caught him red-handed. Little things like compacts and toothpaste and lipsticks. Stuff he can sell easily," the proprietor said.

As she listened Mrs. Higgins looked at Alfred sometimes and nodded her head sadly, and when Sam Carr had finished she said gravely, "Is it so, Alfred?"

"Yes."

"Why have you been doing it?"

"I been spending money, I guess."

"On what?"

"Going around with the guys, I guess," Alfred said.

Mrs. Higgins put out her hand and touched Sam Carr's arm with an understanding gentleness, and speaking as though afraid of disturbing him, she said, "If you would only listen to me before doing anything." Her simple earnestness made her shy; her humility made her falter and look away, but in a moment she was smiling gravely again, and she said with a kind of patient dignity, "What did you intend to do, Mr. Carr?"

"I was going to get a cop. That's what I ought to do."

"Yes, I suppose so. It's not for me to say, because he's my son. Yet I sometimes think a little good advice is the best thing for a boy when he's at a certain period in his life," she said.

Alfred couldn't understand his mother's quiet composure, for if they had been at home and someone had suggested that he was going to be arrested, he knew she would be in a rage and would cry out against him. Yet now she was standing there with that gentle, pleading smile on her face, saying, "I wonder if you don't think it would be better just to let him come home with me. He looks like a big fellow, doesn't he? It takes some of them a long time to get any sense," and they both stared at Alfred, who shifted away with a bit of light shining for a moment on his thin face and the tiny pimples over his cheekbone.

But even while he was turning away uneasily Alfred was realizing that Mr. Carr had become aware that his mother was really a fine woman; he knew that Sam Carr was puzzled by his mother, as if he had expected her to come in and plead with him tearfully, and instead he was being made to feel a bit ashamed by her vast tolerance. While there was only the sound of the mother's soft, assured voice in the store, Mr. Carr began to nod his head encouragingly at her. Without being alarmed, while being just large and still and simple and hopeful, she was becoming dominant there in the dimly lit store. "Of course, I don't want to be harsh," Mr. Carr was saying, "I'll tell you what I'll do. I'll just fire him and let it go at that. How's that?" and he got up and shook hands with Mrs. Higgins, bowing low to her in deep respect.

There was such warmth and gratitude in the way she said, "I'll never forget your kindness," that Mr. Carr began to feel warm and genial himself.

"Sorry we had to meet this way," he said. "But I'm glad I got in touch with you. Just wanted to do the right thing, that's all," he said.

"It's better to meet like this than never, isn't it?" she said. Suddenly they clasped hands as if they liked each other, as if they had known each other a long time. "Good night, sir," she said.

"Good night, Mrs. Higgins. I'm truly sorry," he said.

The mother and son walked along the street together, and the mother was taking a long, firm stride as she looked ahead with her stern face full of worry. Alfred was afraid to speak to her, he was afraid of the silence that was between them, so he only looked ahead too, for the excitement and relief was still pretty strong in him, but in a little while, going along like that in silence made him terribly aware of the strength and the sternness in her; he began to wonder what she was thinking of as she stared ahead so grimly; she seemed to have forgotten that he walked beside her; so when they were passing under the Sixth Avenue elevated and the rumble of the train seemed to break the silence, he said in his old blustering way, "Thank God it turned out like that. I certainly won't get in a jam like that again."

"Be quiet. Don't speak to me. You've disgraced me again and again," she said bitterly.

"That's the last time. That's all I'm saying."

"Have the decency to be quiet," she snapped. They kept on their way, looking straight ahead.

When they were at home and his mother took off her coat, Alfred saw that she was really only half dressed, and she made him feel afraid again when she said, without even looking at him, "You're a bad lot; God forgive you. It's one thing after another and always has been. Why do you stand there stupidly? Go to bed, why don't you?" When he was going, she said, "I'm going to make myself a cup of tea. Mind, now, not a word about tonight to your father."

While Alfred was undressing in his bedroom, he heard his mother moving around the kitchen. She filled the kettle and put it on the stove. She moved a chair. And as he listened there was no shame in him, just wonder and a kind of admiration of her strength and repose. He could still see Sam Carr nodding his head encouragingly to her; he could hear her talking simply and earnestly, and as he sat on his bed he felt a pride in her strength. "She certainly was smooth," he thought. "Gee, I'd like to tell her she sounded swell."

And at last he got up and went along to the kitchen, and when he was at the door he saw his mother pouring herself a cup of tea. He watched and he didn't move. Her face, as she sat there, was a frightened, broken face utterly unlike the face of the woman who had been so assured a little while ago in the drugstore. When she reached out and lifted the kettle to pour hot water in her cup, her hand trembled and the water splashed on the stove. Leaning back in the chair, she sighed and lifted the cup to her lips, and her lips were groping loosely as if they would never reach the cup. She swallowed the hot tea eagerly, and then she straightened up in relief, though the hand holding the cup still trembled. She looked very old.

It seemed to Alfred that this was the way it had been every time he had been in trouble before, that this trembling had really been in her as she hurried out half dressed to the drugstore. He understood why she had sat alone in the kitchen the night his young sister had kept repeating doggedly that she was getting married. Now he felt all that his mother had been thinking of as they walked along the street together a little while ago. He watched his mother, and he never spoke, but at that moment his youth seemed to be over; he knew all the years of her life by the way her hand trembled as she raised the cup to her lips. It seemed to him that this was the first time he had ever looked upon his mother.

Practice

Read each part of the following exercise and answer all **27** questions. Below are four different ways of characterizing an individual. For each of the sentences that follow, indicate the way in which the individual is being characterized by selecting the appropriate **letter**: *A, B, C,* or *D.*

A — Appearance

B — Actions

C — Words

D — Thoughts and Feelings

1. ______ Sam Carr was a little gray-haired man.
2. ______ Alfred buttoned his coat nervously.
3. ______ His heart began to beat so loud it was hard for him to get his breath.
4. ______ His face got red and he knew he looked fierce with indignation.
5. ______ His blue eyes were shining behind his glasses, and his lips moved underneath his gray mustache.
6. ______ "Petty thieving, eh, Alfred?" Sam Carr said.
7. ______ Alfred grew very frightened and he didn't know what to say.
8. ______ "This is the first time I ever took anything," said Alfred.
9. ______ Slowly Alfred dipped into his pocket and took out a blue compact, two tubes of toothpaste, and a lipstick.

10. ______ Ever since Alfred had left school he had been getting into trouble wherever he worked.

11. ______ Alfred began to feel that familiar terror growing in him that had been in him every time he got into such trouble.

12. ______ He wanted to sound like a swaggering, big guy who could look after himself, yet the old, childish hope was in him, the longing that someone at home would come and help him.

13. ______ He longed that she might come before Mr. Carr saw the cop on the beat passing the door.

14. ______ Sam Carr looked hard-faced and stern.

15. ______ Mrs. Higgins was large and plump, with a smile on her friendly face.

16. ______ She acted with a calmness and dignity.

17. ______ Mr. Carr was a little embarrassed by her lack of terror and her simplicity.

18. ______ Mrs. Higgins put out her hand and touched Sam Carr's arm with an understanding gentleness.

19. ______ "I don't want to be harsh," Mr. Carr said.

20. ______ He got up and shook hands with Mrs. Higgins, bowing low to her in deep respect.

21. ______ Her stern face was full of worry.

22. ______ Alfred was afraid to speak to her.

23. ______ He began to wonder what she was thinking of as she stared ahead so grimly.

24. ______ "Be quiet. Don't speak to me. You've disgraced me again and again," she said bitterly.

25. ______ Her face, as she sat there, was a frightened, broken face utterly unlike the face of the woman who had been so assured a little while ago in the drugstore.

26. ______ Leaning back in the chair, she sighed and lifted the cup to her lips.

27. ______ It seemed to him that this was the first time he had ever looked upon his mother.

Score the Practice exercise using the Answer Key, and go on to the Composition part of this guide.

Composition

This part of the guide will help you to apply what you have learned about characterization. Write three separate paragraphs, one for each character in "All the Years of Her Life." Develop each of your paragraphs according to the plan outlined here.

Plan

- Introduce the character by name and tell what role he or she plays in the story.
- Describe the character's appearance.
- What important interactions take place between this character and others in the story?
- What words spoken in the story help us to understand this character? Explain.

- In what way, if any, does the character change by the end of the story?
- How do you feel about this character, and why?

Use the Checklist to help you review and revise your writing. Do this for all drafts and your final copy.

Checklist	**Yes**	**No**
1. I have written three separate paragraphs, one for each character in the story.	_____	_____
2. I introduce each character by name and tell his or her role in the story.	_____	_____
3. I describe each character's appearance and explain the meaning of his or her statements.	_____	_____
4. I describe the important interactions that take place, and show how each character changes.	_____	_____
5. I indicate how I feel about each character, and why.	_____	_____
6. I used transitions to connect ideas and create unity in my writing.	_____	_____
7. I proofread and edited my composition.	_____	_____
8. I wrote a corrected copy of my work.	_____	_____

Submit the completed writing assignment and Practice exercise to your instructor for evaluation.

30.

Creating Characters

The first part of this guide gives you an opportunity to practice your grammar, usage, and punctuation. It can also be used to improve your spelling, learn new words, and sharpen your reading comprehension skills. These activities will help to improve your writing.

Skills Practice

Choose one or more of the following exercises and answer at least **thirty** questions:

A **corrective** exercise recommended by your instructor.

A **spelling** exercise from available materials.

A **vocabulary** exercise from available materials.

A **reading comprehension** exercise from available materials.

Record the number of questions you complete, and score the exercise using available answer keys. Then go on to the Composition part of this guide.

Composition

This guide will help you to develop a character from the story, "All the Years of Her Life." Create a character based on one of the people mentioned in the story: Alfred's father, sister, a brother, or a policeman. Follow the outline presented here to write your essay.

Outline

I. The Introductory Paragraph

   A. State the title and author of the story.

   B. Tell where and when the story takes place. If time is not indicated, assume that the story takes place in the present.

   C. Introduce the original characters by name and tell what role each plays in the story.

   D. Describe the conflict in the story.

II. The Development Paragraph

   A. Introduce your new character by name and tell what role he or she plays in the story.

   B. Describe the character.

   C. What does this character do, and what important interactions take place with others in the story?

   D. What thoughts and feelings does this character have about the situation?

III. The Concluding Paragraph

   A. Does the character influence the outcome of the story? How?

   B. How do you feel about this new character, and why?

Use the Checklist to help you review and revise your writing. Do this for all drafts and your final copy.

Checklist	**Yes**	**No**
1. In my first paragraph I introduce the title and author of the story, the setting, characters, and the conflict.	____	____
2. In my development paragraph, I introduce the new character and describe him or her.	____	____
3. I tell what this character does, what important interactions take place with others in the story, and how the character feels about the situation.	____	____
4. I tell how the character influences the outcome of the story, and how I feel about this character.	____	____
5. I used transitions to connect ideas and create unity in my writing.	____	____
6. I proofread and edited my composition.	____	____
7. I wrote a corrected copy of my work.	____	____

Submit the completed writing assignment and Practice exercise to your instructor for evaluation.

31.

Writing Dialogue

This guide will help you to write dialogue. In a story, **dialogue is conversation between characters.** Through conversation the author can establish the situation, develop characters, present actions and ideas, and express themes. The direct statements of a character are indicated by quotation marks, while indirect statements are not. Both techniques can be used to present the words of a character to the reader.

Direct Quotations

When characters in a story speak, their words have quotation marks around them. The words within these quotation marks are exactly what the character is saying. These are called **direct quotations.**

The girl said, "There's a worm in that peach!"

"I'm going to find another peach," said the father.

The mother asked, "Is your father home?"

Sometimes, another character or the narrator tells us what someone has said. They report the meaning expressed by the speaker, but do not give his or her exact words. This is an **indirect quotation.**

The girl said there was a worm in that peach.

The father said he was going to find another peach.

The mother asked the girl if her father was home.

Dialogue allows the reader to experience firsthand what a character is saying and feeling. The story that follows is created primarily through the use of direct quotations.

"Gaston" is a short story by William Saroyan. Mr. Saroyan, a prominent American author, wrote many novels, plays, and short stories. This story is about a young girl's visit with her father. The author focuses on conversation as a way of telling the story. Read the story, then complete the exercises that follow. Use the dictionary to look up the definition of unfamiliar words.

Gaston

William Saroyan

They were to eat peaches, as planned, after her nap, and now she sat across from the man who would have been a total stranger except that he was in fact her father. They had been together again (although she couldn't quite remember when they had been together before) for almost a hundred years now, or was it only since the day before yesterday? Anyhow, they were together again, and he was kind of funny. First, he had the biggest mustache she had ever seen, although to her it was not a mustache at all; it was a lot of red and brown hair under his nose and around the ends of his mouth. Second, he wore a blue-and-white striped jersey instead of a shirt and tie, and no coat. His arms were covered with the same hair, only it was a little lighter and thinner. He wore blue slacks, but no shoes and socks. He was barefoot, and so was she, of course.

He was at home. She was with him in his home in Paris, if you could call it a home. He was very old, especially for a young man—36, he had told her; and she was six, just up from sleep on a very hot afternoon in August.

That morning, on a little walk in the neighborhood, she had seen peaches in a box outside a small store and she had stopped to look at them, so he had bought a kilo.

Now, the peaches were on a large plate on the card table at which they sat. There were seven of them, but one of them was flawed. It *looked* as good as the others, almost the size of a tennis ball, nice red fading to light green, but where the stem had been there was now a break that went straight down into the heart of the seed.

He placed the biggest and best-looking peach on the small plate in front of the girl, and then took the flawed peach and began to remove the skin. When he had half the skin off the peach he ate that side, neither of them talking, both of them just being there, and not being excited or anything—no plans, that is.

The man held the half-eaten peach and looked down into the cavity, into the open seed. The girl looked, too.

While they were looking, two feelers poked out from the cavity. They were attached to a kind of brown knob-head, which followed the feelers, and then two large legs took a strong grip on the edge of the cavity and hoisted some of the rest of whatever it was out of the seed, and stopped there a moment, as if to look around. The man studied the seed dweller, and so, of course, did the girl.

The creature paused only a fraction of a second, and then continued to come out of the seed, to walk down the eaten side of the peach to wherever it was going.

The girl had never seen anything like it—a whole big thing made out of brown color, a knob-head, feelers, and a great many legs. It was very active, too. Almost businesslike, you might say.

The man placed the peach back on the plate. The creature moved off the peach onto the surface of the white plate. There it came to a thoughtful stop.

"Who is it?" the girl said.

"Gaston."

"Where does he live?"

"Well, he *used* to live in this peach seed, but now that the peach has been harvested and sold, and I have eaten half of it, it looks as if he's out of house and home."

"Aren't you going to squash him?"

"No, of course not, why should I?"

"He's a bug. He's *ugh*."

"Not at all. He's Gaston the grand boulevardier."

"Everybody hollers when a bug comes out of an apple, but you don't holler or *anything*."

"Of course not. How would *we* like it if somebody hollered every time we came out of our house?"

"Why *would* they?"

"Precisely. So why should we holler at Gaston?"

"He's not the same as us."

"Well, not exactly, but he's the same as a lot of other occupants of peach seeds. Now, the poor fellow hasn't got a home, and there he is with all that pure design and handsome form, and nowhere to go."

"Handsome?"

"Gaston is just about the handsomest of his kind I've ever seen."

"What's he saying?"

"Well, he's a little confused. Now, inside that house of his he had everything in order. Bed here, porch there, and so forth."

"Show me."

The man picked up the peach, leaving Gaston entirely alone on the white plate. He removed the peeling and ate the rest of the peach.

"Nobody else I know would do that," the girl said. "They'd throw it away."

"I can't imagine why. It's a perfectly good peach." He opened the seed and placed the two sides not far from Gaston. The girl studied the open halves.

"Is *that* where he lives?"

"It's where he used to live. Gaston is out in the world and on his own now. You can see for yourself how comfortable he was in there. He had everything."

"Now what has he got?"

"Not very much, I'm afraid."

"What's he going to do?"

"What are *we* going to do?"

"Well, we're not going to squash him, that's one thing we're *not* going to do," the girl said.

"What *are* we going to do, then?"

"Put him back?"

"Oh *that* house is finished."

"Well, he can't live in our house, can he?"

"Not happily."

"Can he live in our house *at all*?"

"Well, he could *try*, I suppose. Don't you want a peach?"

"Only if it's a peach with somebody in the seed."

"Well, see if you can find a peach that has an opening at the top, because if you can, that'll be a peach in which you're likeliest to find somebody."

The girl examined each of the peaches on the big plate.

"They're all shut," she said.

"Well, eat one, then."

"No. I want the same kind that you ate, with somebody in the seed."

"Well, to tell you the truth, the peach I ate would be considered a bad peach, so of course stores don't like to sell them. I was sold that one by mistake, most likely. And so now Gaston is without a home, and we've got six perfect peaches to eat."

"I don't want a perfect peach. I want one with people."

"Well, I'll go out and see if I can find one."

"Where will I go?"

"You'll go with me, unless you'd rather stay. I'll only be five minutes."

"If the phone rings, what shall I say?"

"I don't think it'll ring, but if it does, say hello and see who it is."

"If it's my mother, what shall I say?"

"Tell her I've gone to get you a bad peach, and anything else you want to tell her."

"If she wants me to go back, what shall I say?"

"Say yes if you want to go back."

"Do you want me to?"

"Of course not, but the important thing is what you want, not what I want."

"Why is *that* the important thing?"

"Because I want you to be where you want to be."

"I want to be here."

"I'll be right back."

He put on socks and shoes, and a jacket, and went out. She watched Gaston trying to find out what to do next. Gaston wandered around the plate, but everything seemed wrong and he didn't know what to do or where to go.

The telephone rang, and her mother said she was sending the chauffeur to pick her up because there was a little party for somebody's daughter who was also six, and then tomorrow, they would fly back to New York.

"Let me speak to your father," she said.

"He's gone to get a peach."

"*One* peach?"

"One with people."

"You haven't been with your father two days and already you *sound* like him."

"There *are* peaches with people in them. I know. I saw one of them come out."

"A bug?"

"Not a bug. Gaston."

"*Who*?"

"Gaston the grand something."

"Somebody else gets a peach with a bug in it, and throws it away, but not him. He makes up a lot of foolishness about it."

"It is not foolishness."

"All right, all right, don't get angry at me about a horrible peach bug of some kind."

"Gaston is right here, just outside his broken house, and I'm not angry at you."

"You'll have a lot of fun at the party."

"OK."

"Are you glad you saw your father?"

"Of course I am."

"Is he funny?"

"Yes."

"Is he crazy?"

"Yes. I mean, no. He doesn't holler when he sees a bug crawling out of a peach seed or anything. He just looks at it carefully. But it *is* just a bug, isn't it *really*?"

"That's all it is."

"And we'll *have* to squash it?"

"That's right. I can't wait to see you, darling. These two days have been like two years to me. Good-bye."

The girl watched Gaston on the plate, and she actually didn't like him. He was all *ugh*, as he had been in the first place. He didn't have a home anymore and he was wandering around on the white plate and he was silly and wrong and ridiculous and useless and all sorts of other things. She cried a little, but only inside, because long ago she had decided she didn't like crying because if you ever started to cry it seemed as if there was so much to cry about you almost couldn't stop, and she didn't like that at all. The open halves of the peach seed were wrong, too. They were ugly or something. They weren't clean.

The man bought a kilo of peaches but found no flawed peaches among them, so he bought another kilo at another store, and this time there were *two* that were flawed. He hurried back to his flat and let himself in.

His daughter was in her room, in her best dress.

"My mother phoned," she said, "and she's sending the chauffeur for me because there's another birthday party."

"Another?"

"I mean, there's *always* a lot of them in New York."

"Will the chauffeur bring you back?"

"No. We're flying back to New York tomorrow."

"Oh."

"I liked being in your house."

"I liked having you here."

"Why do you live here?"

"This is my home."

"It's nice, but it's a lot different from our home."

"Yes, I suppose it is."

"It's kind of like Gaston's house."

"Where *is* Gaston?"

"I squashed him."

"Really? Why?"

"Everybody squashes bugs and worms."

"Oh. Well. I found you a peach."

"I don't want a peach anymore."

"OK."

He got her dressed, and he was packing her stuff when the chauffeur arrived. He went down the three flights of stairs with his daughter and the chauffeur, and in the street he was about to hug the girl when he decided he had better not. They shook hands instead, like strangers.

He watched the huge car drive off, then he went around the corner where he took coffee every morning, feeling a little, he thought, like Gaston on the white plate.

Practice

Read each part of the following exercise and answer all **19** questions. Begin with the five rules for writing dialogue, *A* through *E*, and accompanying examples.

A. In a direct quote, the words of the speaker are indicated by quotation marks. The first word of the quotation is capitalized.

> The girl said, "Everybody squashes bugs and worms."

B. The speaker's words are set off from the rest of the sentence by a comma.

> The girl said, "He's not the same as us."
>
> "He's not the same as us," the girl said.

C. End punctuation for quotations that make a statement, ask a question, or express excitement, appear inside the quotation mark.

> "Gaston is just about the handsomest of his kind."
>
> "Aren't you going to squash him?" asked the girl.
>
> "Watch out for that bug!" she screamed.

D. Both parts of a divided quote are set off by commas and enclosed in quotation marks. The two parts of the divided quote below make one complete sentence.

> "Gaston is out in the world," the father said, "and on his own now."

E. If the second part of a divided quote is a new sentence, it begins with a capital letter.

> "Gaston is out in the world," the father said. "He's on his own now."

Apply the rules you have just learned to complete the exercise that follows. Rewrite each sentence, adding the punctuation, quotation marks, and capital letters where appropriate.

1. look at the creature coming out of the peach said the girl

    ____

2. the father said that's where Gaston lives

    ____

3. he's ugly exclaimed the girl

    ____

4. he's quite handsome for his kind replied the father

    ____

5. where will Gaston live now asked the girl

    ____

6. Gaston is out in the world answered the father and on his own now

    ____

7. I want a peach said the girl only if somebody is in the seed

    ____

8. I think you like Gaston said the father I'll try to get you another peach just like that one

    ____

9. the girl's mother said let me speak to your father

    ____

10. he's not here said the girl he's gone to get me a peach

    ____

11. is he getting you just one peach asked the mother

    ____

12. the girl answered he's going to find me a peach with people in it

____

13. the mother asked the girl is your father funny

____

14. he doesn't holler when he sees a bug crawling out of a peach said the girl

____

15. where is Gaston asked the father when he returned

____

16. I squashed him the girl replied

____

17. why did you do that he asked

____

18. I don't want a peach any more said the girl sadly

____

19. I feel a little bit like Gaston said the father

____

Score the Practice exercise using the Answer Key, and go on to the Composition part of this guide.

Composition

This part of the guide will help you apply what you have learned about writing dialogue. In the story "Gaston," the mother and the father never communicate directly. Create a conversation between these two characters by following the plan outlined below.

Plan

- Write a paragraph in which you introduce the mother and father and tell how each views the other.
- Create a conversation between the mother and father that contains at least five exchanges. An exchange occurs when one person says something and the other responds.
- Write a paragraph in which you summarize how each character feels when the conversation ends.

Use the Checklist to help you review and revise your writing. Do this for all drafts and your final copy.

Checklist	Yes	No
1. I wrote a paragraph in which I introduce the characters and tell how each views the other.	_____	_____
2. I created a conversation between the mother and father that contains five exchanges.	_____	_____
3. I wrote a paragraph that summarizes how each character feels when the conversation ends.	_____	_____
4. I used transitions to connect ideas and create unity in my writing.	_____	_____
5. I proofread and edited my composition.	_____	_____
6. I wrote a corrected copy of my work.	_____	_____

Submit the completed writing assignment and Practice exercise to your instructor for evaluation.

32.

Conflict and Plot: A

This guide will help you to understand the use of conflict and plot in literature. **A conflict is a struggle between opposing forces.** All stories have a conflict, a major problem that involves the characters. Complications in the plot create tension and further conflict.

Every **plot—the events in a story**—is built around conflict in order to create interest and build suspense. Readers want to know how characters react to conflict and how the story ends.

Conflict

Conflict in literature can take several forms. A character may struggle against another character, against society, against oneself, against nature, or against the unknown. Often, more than one conflict is apparent.

1. **Conflict with others** sets one character against another and is the most basic kind of conflict.

2. **Conflict with society** sets one character against accepted ways of thinking and behaving. Since society is made up of people, this is conflict between people on a larger scale.

3. **Conflict with self** involves a struggle that takes place within a character. It occurs when an individual is confronted with a difficult choice or an unpleasant situation.

4. **Conflict with nature** sets a character against the forces of nature.

5. **Conflict with the unknown** sets a character against that which is beyond human comprehension such as: fate, magic, or death.

Plot

The plot is a series of events in a story through which the author reveals what is happening, to whom, and why. It is a plan of action that adds dimension by telling why something has happened. The author builds tension through the development of the plot. All plots follow a basic pattern like the one shown below in the chart.

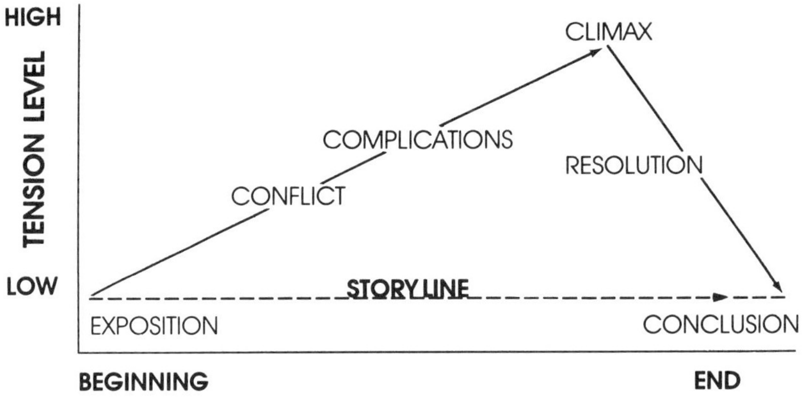

The plot includes the exposition, conflict, complications, the climax, the resolution, and a conclusion.

- The **exposition** is the beginning part of the plot in which the setting, characters, and background information are introduced.
- **Conflict** is a struggle between opposing forces in the story.
- **Complications** are twists and turns in the plot which create tension and further conflict.
- The **climax** is the point of greatest tension in the story.
- The **resolution** refers to those events which follow the climax of the story and lead to the conclusion.
- The **conclusion** is how the story ends.

A **story line** is a listing of the events that occur, from beginning to end.

- A family friend comes to visit.
- He brings a monkey's paw with him.
- The paw is magical; its owner has three wishes.
- The father uses all three wishes.

We are told who and what is involved, but not **why** any of this has happened. A story line, by itself, is one-dimensional and uninteresting because it creates no tension.

"The Monkey's Paw" is a short story by W. W. Jacobs, a British writer. The story takes place in England around 1900. Stories of suspense such as this one focus on plot development. The primary conflict in this story is between man and the unknown. Read the story, then complete the exercises that follow. Use the dictionary to look up the definition of unfamiliar words.

The Monkey's Paw

W. W. Jacobs

Without, the night was cold and wet, but in the small parlor of Lakesnam Villa the blinds were drawn and the fire burned brightly. Father and son were at chess, the former, who possessed ideas about the game involving radical changes, putting his king into such sharp and unnecessary perils that it even provoked comment from the white-haired old lady knitting placidly by the fire.

"Hark at the wind," said Mr. White, who, having seen a fatal mistake after it was too late, was amiably desirous of preventing his son from seeing it.

"I'm listening," said the latter, grimly surveying the board as he stretched out his hand. "Check."

"I should hardly think that he'd come tonight," said his father, with his hand poised over the board.

"Mate," replied the son.

"That's the worst of living so far out," bawled Mr. White, with sudden and unlooked-for violence; "of all the beastly, slushy, out-of-the-way places to live in, this is the worst. Pathway's a bog, and the road's a torrent. I don't know what people are thinking about. I suppose because only two houses on the road are let, they think it doesn't matter."

"Never mind, dear," said his wife soothingly; "perhaps you'll win the next one."

Mr. White looked up sharply, just in time to intercept a knowing glance between mother and son. The words died away on his lips, and he hid a guilty grin in his thin gray beard.

"There he is," said Herbert White, as the gate banged loudly and heavy footsteps came toward the door.

The old man rose with hospitable haste, and opening the door, was heard condoling with the new arrival. The new arrival also condoled with himself, so that Mrs. White said, "Tut, tut!" and coughed gently as her husband entered the room, followed by a tall burly man, beady of eye and rubicund of visage.

"Sergeant-Major Morris," he said, introducing him.

The sergeant-major shook hands, and taking the proffered seat by the fire, watched contentedly while his host got out whisky and tumblers and stood a small copper kettle on the fire.

At the third glass his eyes got brighter, and he began to talk, the little family circle regarding with eager interest this visitor from distant parts, as he squared his broad shoulders in the chair and spoke of strange scenes and doughty deeds, of wars and plagues and strange peoples.

"Twenty-one years of it," said Mr. White, nodding at his wife and son. "When he went away he was a slip of a youth in the warehouse. Now look at him."

"He don't look to have taken much harm," said Mrs. White politely.

"I'd like to go to India myself," said the old man, "just to look round a bit, you know."

"Better where you are," said the sergeant-major, shaking his head. He put down the empty glass and, sighing softly, shook it again.

"I should like to see those old temples and fakirs and jugglers," said the old man. "What was that you started telling me the other day about a monkey's paw or something, Morris?"

"Nothing," said the soldier hastily. "Leastways, nothing worth hearing."

"Monkey's paw?" said Mrs. White curiously.

"Well, it's just a bit of what you might call magic, perhaps," said the sergeant-major off-handedly.

His three listeners leaned forward eagerly. The visitor absentmindedly put his empty glass to his lips and then set it down again. His host filled it for him.

"To look at," said the sergeant-major, fumbling in his pocket, "it's just an ordinary little paw, dried to a mummy."

He took something out of his pocket and proffered it. Mrs. White drew back with a grimace, but her son, taking it, examined it curiously.

"And what is there special about it?" inquired Mr. White, as he took it from his son and, having examined it, placed it upon the table.

"It had a spell put on it by an old fakir," said the sergeant-major, "a very holy man. He wanted to show that fate ruled people's lives, and that those who interfered with it did so to their sorrow. He put a spell on it so that three separate men could each have three wishes from it."

His manner was so impressive that his hearers were conscious that their light laughter jarred somewhat.

"Well, why don't you have three, sir?" said Herbert White cleverly.

The soldier regarded him in the way that middle age is wont to regard presumptuous youth. "I have," he said quietly, and his blotchy face whitened.

"And did you really have the three wishes granted?" asked Mrs. White.

"I did," said the sergeant-major, and his glass tapped against his strong teeth.

"And has anybody else wished?" inquired the old lady.

"The first man had his three wishes, yes," was the reply. "I don't know what the first two were, but the third was for death. That's how I got the paw."

His tones were so grave that a hush fell upon the group.

"If you've had your three wishes, it's no good to you now, then, Morris," said the old man at last. "What do you keep it for?"

The soldier shook his head. "Fancy, I suppose," he said slowly. "I did have some idea of selling it, but I don't think I will. It has caused enough mischief already. Besides, people won't buy. They think it's a fairy tale, some of them, and those who do think anything of it want to try it first and pay me afterward."

"If you could have another three wishes," said the old man, eyeing him keenly, "would you have them?"

"I don't know," said the other. "I don't know."

He took the paw, and dangling it between his front finger and thumb, suddenly threw it upon the fire. White, with a slight cry, stooped down and snatched it off.

"Better let it burn," said the soldier solemnly.

"If you don't want it, Morris," said the old man, "give it to me."

"I won't," said his friend doggedly. "I threw it on the fire. If you keep it, don't blame me for what happens. Pitch it on the fire again, like a sensible man."

The other shook his head and examined his new possession closely. "How do you do it?" he inquired.

"Hold it up in your right hand and wish aloud," said the sergeant-major, "but I warn you of the consequences."

"Sounds like the *Arabian Nights*," said Mrs. White, as she rose and began to set the supper. "Don't you think you might wish for four pairs of hands for me?"

Her husband drew the talisman from his pocket and then all three burst into laughter as the sergeant-major, with a look of alarm on his face, caught him by the arm. "If you must wish," he said gruffly, "wish for something sensible."

Mr. White dropped it back into his pocket, and placing chairs, motioned his friend to the table. In the business of supper the talisman was partly forgotten, and afterward the three sat listening in an entralled fashion to a second installment of the soldier's adventures in India.

"If the tale about the monkey paw is not more truthful than those he has been telling us," said Herbert, as the door closed behind their guest, just in time for him to catch the last train, "we shan't make much out of it."

"Did you give him anything for it, father?" inquired Mrs. White, regarding her husband closely.

"A trifle," said he, coloring slightly. "He didn't want it, but I made him take it. And he pressed me again to throw it away."

"Likely," said Herbert, with pretended horror. "Why, we're going to be rich, and famous, and happy. Wish to be an emperor, father, to begin with; then you can't be henpecked."

He darted round the table, pursued by the maligned Mrs. White armed with an antimacassar.

Mr. White took the paw from his pocket and eyed it dubiously. "I don't know what to wish for, and that's a fact," he said slowly. "It seems to me I've got all I want."

"If you only cleared the house, you'd be quite happy, wouldn't you?" said Herbert, with his hand on his shoulder. "Well, wish for two hundred pounds, then; that'll just do it."

His father, smiling shamefacedly at his own credulity, held up the talisman, as his son, with a solemn face somewhat marred by a wink at his mother, sat down at the piano and struck a few impressive chords.

"I wish for two hundred pounds," said the old man distinctly.

A fine crash from the piano greeted the words, interrupted by a shuddering cry from the old man. His wife and son ran toward him.

"It moved," he cried, with a glance of disgust at the object as it lay on the floor. "As I wished it twisted in my hands like a snake."

"Well, I don't see the money," said his son, as he picked it up and placed it on the table, "and I bet I never shall."

"It must have been your fancy, father," said his wife, regarding him anxiously.

He shook his head. "Never mind, though; there's no harm done, but it gave me a shock all the same."

They sat down by the fire again while the two men finished their pipes. Outside, the wind was higher than ever, and the old man started nervously at the sound of a door banging upstairs. A silence unusual and depressing settled upon all three, which lasted until the old couple rose to retire for the night.

"I expect you'll find the cash tied up in a big bag in the middle of your bed," said Herbert, as he bade them good night, "and something horrible squatting up on top of the wardrobe watching you as you pocket your ill-gotten gains."

In the brightness of the wintry sun next morning as it streamed over the breakfast table Herbert laughed at his fears. There was an air of prosaic wholesomeness about the room which it had lacked on the previous night, and the dirty, shriveled little paw was pitched on the sideboard with a carelessness which betokened no great belief in its virtues.

"I suppose all old soldiers are the same," said Mrs. White. "The idea of our listening to such nonsense! How could wishes be granted in these days? And if they could, how could two hundred pounds hurt you, father?"

"Might drop on his head from the sky," said the frivolous Herbert.

"Morris said the things happened so naturally," said his father, "that you might if you so wished attribute it to coincidence."

"Well, don't break into the money before I come back," said Herbert, as he rose from the table. "I'm afraid it'll turn you into a mean, avaricious man, and we shall have to disown you."

His mother laughed, and following him to the door, watched him down the road, and returning to the breakfast table, was very happy at the expense of her husband's credulity. All of which did not prevent her from scurrying to the door at the postman's knock, nor prevent her from referring somewhat shortly to retired sergeant-majors of bibulous habits when she found that the post brought a tailor's bill.

"Herbert will have some more of his funny remarks, I expect, when he comes home," she said, as they sat at dinner.

"I dare say," said Mr. White, pouring himself out some beer; "but for all that, the thing moved in my hand; that I'll swear to."

"You thought it did," said the old lady soothingly.

"I say it did," replied the other. "There was no thought about it; I had just—What's the matter?"

His wife made no reply. She was watching the mysterious movements of a man outside, who, peering in an undecided fashion at the house, appeared to be trying to make up his mind to enter. In mental connection with the two hundred pounds, she noticed that the stranger was well dressed and wore a silk hat of glossy newness. Three times he paused at the gate, and then walked on again. The fourth time he stood with his hand upon it, and then with sudden resolution flung it open and walked up the path. Mrs. White at the same moment placed her hands behind her, and hurriedly unfastening the strings of her apron, put that useful article of apparel beneath the cushion of her chair.

She brought the stranger, who seemed ill at ease, into the room. He gazed furtively at Mrs. White, and listened in preoccupied fashion as the old lady apologized for the appearance of the room, and her husband's coat, a garment which he usually reserved for the garden. She then waited as patiently as her sex would permit for him to broach his business, but he was at first strangely silent.

"I—was asked to call," he said at last, and stooped and picked a piece of cotton from his trousers. "I come from Maw and Meggins."

The old lady started. "Is anything the matter?" she asked breathlessly. "Has anything happened to Herbert? What is it? What is it?"

Her husband interposed. "There, there, mother," he said hastily. "Sit down, and don't jump to conclusions. You've not brought bad news, I'm sure, sir," and he eyed the other wistfully.

"I'm sorry—" began the visitor.

"Is he hurt?" demanded the mother.

The visitor bowed in assent. "Badly hurt," he said quietly, "but he is not in any pain."

"Oh, thank God!" said the old woman, clasping her hands. "Thank God for that! Thank – –"

She broke off suddenly as the sinister meaning of the assurance dawned upon her and she saw the awful confirmation of her fears in the other's averted face. She caught her breath, and turning to her slower witted husband, laid her trembling old hand upon his. There was a long silence.

"He was caught in the machinery," said the visitor at length, in a low voice.

"Caught in the machinery," repeated Mr. White, in a dazed fashion, "yes."

He sat staring blankly out at the window, and taking his wife's hand between his own, pressed it as he had been wont to do in their old courting days nearly forty years before.

"He was the only one left to us," he said, turning gently to the visitor. "It is hard."

The other coughed, and rising, walked slowly to the window. "The firm wished me to convey their sincere sympathy with you in your great loss," he said, without looking around. "I beg that you will understand I am only their servant and merely obeying orders."

There was no reply; the old woman's face was white, her eyes staring, and her breath inaudible; on the husband's face was a look such as his friend the sergeant might have carried into his first action.

"I was to say that Maw and Meggins disclaim all responsibility," continued the other. "They admit no liability at all, but in consideration of your son's services they wish to present you with a certain sum as compensation."

Mr. White dropped his wife's hand, and rising to his feet, gazed with a look of horror at his visitor. His dry lips shaped the words, "How much?"

"Two hundred pounds," was the answer.

Unconscious of his wife's shriek, the old man smiled faintly, put out his hands like a sightless man, and dropped, a senseless heap, to the floor.

In the huge new cemetery, some two miles distant, the old people buried their dead, and came back to a house steeped in shadow and silence. It was all over so quickly that at first they could hardly realize it, and remained in a state of expectation as though of something else to happen—something else which was to lighten this load, too heavy for old hearts to bear. But the days passed, and expectation gave place to resignation—the hopeless resignation of the old, sometimes miscalled apathy. Sometimes they hardly exchanged a word, for now they had nothing to talk about, and their days were long to weariness.

It was about a week after that that the old man, waking suddenly in the night, stretched out his hand and found himself alone. The room was in darkness, and the sound of subdued weeping came from the window. He raised himself in bed and listened.

"Come back," he said tenderly. "You will be cold."

"It is colder for my son," said the old woman, and wept afresh.

The sound of her sobs died away on his ears. The bed was warm, and his eyes heavy with sleep. He dozed fitfully, and then slept until a sudden wild cry from his wife awoke him with a start.

"The monkey's paw!" she cried wildly. "The monkey's paw!"

He started up in alarm. "Where? Where is it? What's the matter?"

She came stumbling across the room toward him. "I want it," she said quietly. "You've not destroyed it?"

"It's in the parlor, on the bracket," he replied, marveling. "Why?"

She cried and laughed together, and bending over, kissed his cheek.

"I only just thought of it," she said hysterically. "Why didn't I think of it before? Why didn't you think of it?"

"Think of what?" he questioned.

"The other two wishes," she replied rapidly. "We've only had one."

"Was not that enough?" he demanded fiercely.

"No," she cried triumphantly; "we'll have one more. Go down and get it quickly, and wish our boy alive again."

The man sat up in bed and flung the bedclothes from his quaking limbs. "Good God, you are mad!" he cried, aghast.

"Get it," she panted; "get it quickly, and wish—Oh, my boy, my boy!"

Her husband struck a match and lit the candle. "Get back to bed," he said unsteadily. "You don't know what you are saying."

"We had the first wish granted," said the old woman feverishly; "why not the second?"

"A coincidence," stammered the old man.

"Go and get it and wish," cried the old woman, and dragged him toward the door.

He went down in the darkness, and felt his way to the parlor, and then to the mantelpiece. The talisman was in its place, and a horrible fear that the unspoken wish might bring his mutilated son before him ere he could escape from the room seized upon him, and he caught his breath as he found that he had lost the direction of the door. His brow cold with sweat, he felt his way round the table, and groped along the wall until he found himself in the small passage with the unwholesome thing in his hand.

Even his wife's face seemed changed as he entered the room. It was white and expectant, and to his fears seemed to have an unnatural look upon it. He was afraid of her.

"Wish!" she cried, in a strong voice.

"It is foolish and wicked," he faltered.

"Wish!" repeated his wife.

He raised his hand. "I wish my son alive again."

The talisman fell to the floor, and he regarded it shudderingly. Then he sank trembling into a chair as the old woman, with burning eyes, walked to the window and raised the blind.

He sat until he was chilled with the cold, glancing occasionally at the figure of the old woman peering through the window. The candle end, which had burnt below the rim of the china candlestick, was throwing pulsating shadows on the ceiling and walls, until, with a flicker larger than the rest, it expired. The old man, with an unspeakable sense of relief at the failure of the talisman, crept back to his bed, and a minute or two afterward the old woman came silently and apathetically beside him.

Neither spoke, but both lay silently listening to the ticking of the clock. A stair creaked, and a squeeky mouse scurried noisily through the wall. The darkness was oppressive, and after lying for some time screwing up his courage, the husband took the box of matches, and striking one, went downstairs for a candle.

At the foot of the stairs the match went out, and he paused to strike another, and at the same moment a knock, so quiet and stealthy as to be scarcely audible, sounded on the front door.

The matches fell from his hand. He stood motionless, his breath suspended until the knock was repeated. Then he turned and fled swiftly back to his room, and closed the door behind him. A third knock sounded through the house.

"What's that?" cried the old woman, starting up.

"A rat," said the old man, in shaking tones—"a rat. It passed me on the stairs."

His wife sat up in bed listening. A loud knock resounded through the house.

"It's Herbert!" she screamed. "It's Herbert!"

She ran to the door, but her husband was before her, and catching her by the arm, held her tightly.

"What are you going to do?" he whispered hoarsely.

"It's my boy; it's Herbert!" she cried, struggling mechanically. "I forgot it was two miles away. What are you holding me for? Let go. I must open the door."

"For God's sake don't let him in," cried the old man, trembling.

"You're afraid of your own son," she cried, struggling. "Let me go. I'm coming, Herbert; I'm coming."

There was another knock, and another. The old woman with a sudden wrench broke free and ran from the room. Her husband followed to the landing, and called after her appealingly as she hurried downstairs. He heard the chain rattle back and the bottom bolt drawn slowly and stiffly from the socket. Then the old woman's voice, strained and panting.

"The bolt," she cried loudly. "Come down. I can't reach it."

But her husband was on his hands and knees groping wildly on the floor in search of the paw. If he could only find it before the thing outside got in. A perfect fusillade of knocks reverberated through the house, and he heard the scraping of a chair as his wife put it down in the passage against the door. He heard the creaking of the bolt as it came slowly back, and at the same moment, he found the monkey's paw, and frantically breathed his third and last wish.

The knocking ceased suddenly, although the echoes of it were still in the house. He heard the chair drawn back and the door opened. A cold wind rushed up the staircase, and a long loud wail of disappointment and misery from his wife gave him courage to run down to her side, and then to the gate beyond. The street lamp flickering opposite shone on a quiet and deserted road.

Practice

Read each part of the following exercise and answer all **40** questions. Below is a list of the five forms of conflict that are used in literature. Match each passage with the form of conflict it expresses by choosing the appropriate **letter**: *A, B, C, D,* or *E.*

A — Conflict with others

B — Conflict with society

C — Conflict with self

D — Conflict with nature

E — Conflict with the unknown

1. ______ Once I heard the teacher say, "If Aaron were white he might, someday, become President."

2. ______ The father planned to spend more time with the girl, but the mother made other arrangements for her.

3. ______ "You're a bad lot. God forgive you. It's one thing after another and always has been," said Alfred's mother.

4. ______ The fakir put a spell on the paw so that three men could each have three wishes.

5. ______ "Of all the beastly, slushy, out-of-the-way places to live in, this is the worst. Pathway's a bog, and the road's a torrent."

6. ______ "I don't know what to wish for, and that's a fact," he said slowly. "It seems to me I've got all I want."

A — Conflict with others

B — Conflict with society

C — Conflict with self

D — Conflict with nature

E — Conflict with the unknown

7. ______ Her hands trembled, and her face looked old and broken. In her life, she came last.

8. ______ "Th' principal said a colored person have jes as much right paintin' Jesus black as a white person have paintin' him white," said Aaron.

9. ______ The principal answered the angry supervisor by saying, "The artists of all other races have painted whatsoever God they worship to resemble themselves. I see no reason why we should be immune from that privilege."

10. ______ "You're lying to me, Alfred!" said Sam Carr. "What kind of sap do I look like, huh?"

11. ______ "If you keep the paw, don't blame me for what happens. Pitch it on the fire like a sensible man."

12. ______ Three times he paused at the gate, and then walked on again. The fourth time he stood with his hand upon it, and with sudden resolution flung it open and walked up the path.

13. ______ The little girl didn't know whether to stay with her father, or leave.

14. ______ The supervisor coughed and his eyes bulged. He said, "You are not being paid to teach such things in this school, and I am demanding your resignation for overstepping your limit as principal."

15. ______ The husband and wife argued about whether or not to make a second wish with the monkey's paw.

16. ______ "Hold it up in your right hand, and wish aloud," said the Sergeant-Major, "but I warn you of the consequences."

17. ______ "It's my boy; it's Herbert!" she cried. "What are you holding me for? Let go. I must open the door."

18. ______ Alfred began to feel that familiar terror growing in him that had been there every time he got into trouble.

The sentences below and on the next page represent parts of the plot in "The Monkey's Paw." Order them as they occur in the story. Write the **letter** of the first sentence next to number 19, the letter of the second sentence next to number 20, etc.

19. ______	20. ______	21. ______	22. ______
23. ______	24. ______	25. ______	26. ______
27. ______	28. ______	29. ______	

A. "I wish for two hundred pounds," said the old man distinctly.
B. "Herbert was caught in the machinery and is dead. The company wishes to compensate you with two hundred pounds."
C. He found the monkey's paw, and frantically breathed his third and last wish.
D. The street lamp flickering outside shone on a quiet and deserted road.

E. Father and son played chess, while the mother knitted by the fire.

F. He wanted to show that fate ruled people's lives, and those who interfered with it did so to their sorrow.

G. In the small parlor of Lakesnam Villa the blinds were drawn and the fire burned brightly.

H. Sergeant-Major Morris was a tall burly man who had recently returned from India.

I. "If you keep it, don't blame me for what happens. Pitch it on the fire like a sensible man."

J. "We've got two more wishes. Let's wish our boy alive again!"

K. The knocking ceased suddenly, although the echoes of it were still in the house.

Now that you have reordered these sentences, identify the part of the plot to which each belongs. Place the **letter** of the first sentence in the blank next to number 30. Then write in the part of the plot to which it belongs. Do this for each sentence, in order. The first one is done for you.

- The **exposition** is the beginning part of the plot in which the setting, characters, and background information are introduced.
- **Conflict** is a struggle between opposing forces in the story.
- **Complications** are twists and turns in the plot which create tension and further conflict.

- The **climax** is the point of greatest tension in the story.
- The **resolution** refers to those events which follow the climax of the story and lead to the conclusion.
- The **conclusion** is how the story ends.

30. __**G**__ __**exposition**__

31. ______ ____________________

32. ______ ____________________

33. ______ ____________________

34. ______ ____________________

35. ______ ____________________

36. ______ ____________________

37. ______ ____________________

38. ______ ____________________

39. ______ ____________________

40. ______ ____________________

Score the Practice exercise using the Answer Key, and go on to the Composition part of this guide.

Composition

This part of the guide will help you apply what you have learned about conflict and plot. Write a three paragraph essay about "The Monkey's Paw." Follow the outline presented here to write your essay.

Outline

I. The Introductory Paragraph

A. State the title and author of the story.

B. Tell where and when the story takes place.

C. Introduce the important (main) characters.

D. State the form of conflict in this story.

II. The Development Paragraph

A. How is the conflict introduced in the story?

B. What complications occur in the plot?

C. What is the point of greatest tension in the story?

D. How is the conflict resolved?

III. The Concluding Paragraph

A. How does the story end?

B. How do you feel about the outcome of the story, and why?

Use the Checklist to help you review and revise your writing. Do this for all drafts and your final copy.

Checklist	**Yes**	**No**
1. In my first paragraph I introduce the title and author of the story, the setting, the narrator, characters, and the conflict.	____	____
2. In my development paragraph I indicate how the conflict began, what complications occur in the plot, the climax, and how the conflict is resolved.	____	____
3. In my concluding paragraph, I tell how the story ends and how I feel about the outcome.	____	____
4. I used transitions to connect ideas and create unity in my writing.	____	____
5. I proofread and edited my composition.	____	____
6. I wrote a corrected copy of my work.	____	____

Submit the completed writing assignment and Practice exercise to your instructor for evaluation.

33.

Conflict and Plot: B

The first part of this guide gives you an opportunity to practice your grammar, usage, and punctuation. It can also be used to improve your spelling, learn new words, and sharpen your reading comprehension skills. These activities will help to improve your writing.

Skills Practice

Choose one or more of the following exercises and answer at least **thirty** questions:

A **corrective** exercise recommended by your instructor.

A **spelling** exercise from available materials.

A **vocabulary** exercise from available materials.

A **reading comprehension** exercise from available materials.

Record the number of questions you complete, and score the exercise using available answer keys. Then go on to the Composition part of this guide.

Composition

This section of the guide provides additional practice in writing about conflict and plot. Choose a short story to read from available book titles. Write a three paragraph essay by following the outline presented here.

Outline

I. The Introductory Paragraph

A. State the title and author of the story.

B. Tell where and when the story takes place.

C. Introduce the important (main) characters.

D. State the form of conflict in this story.

II. The Development Paragraph

A. How is the conflict introduced in the story?

B. What complications occur in the plot?

C. What is the point of greatest tension in the story?

D. How is the conflict resolved?

III. The Concluding Paragraph

A. How does the story end?

B. How do you feel about the outcome of the story, and why?

Use the Checklist to help you review and revise your writing. Do this for all drafts and your final copy.

Checklist	Yes	No
1. In my first paragraph I introduce the title and author of the story, the setting, the narrator, characters, and the conflict.	____	____
2. In my development paragraph I indicate how the conflict began, what complications occur in the plot, the climax, and how the conflict is resolved.	____	____
3. In my concluding paragraph, I tell how the story ends and how I feel about the outcome.	____	____
4. I used transitions to connect ideas and create unity in my writing.	____	____
5. I proofread and edited my composition.	____	____
6. I wrote a corrected copy of my work.	____	____

Submit the completed writing assignment and Practice exercise to your instructor for evaluation.

34.

Creating Endings

The first part of this guide gives you an opportunity to practice your grammar, usage, and punctuation. It can also be used to improve your spelling, learn new words, and sharpen your reading comprehension skills. These activities will help to improve your writing.

Skills Practice

Choose one or more of the following exercises and answer at least **thirty** questions:

A **corrective** exercise recommended by your instructor.

A **spelling** exercise from available materials.

A **vocabulary** exercise from available materials.

A **reading comprehension** exercise from available materials.

Record the number of questions you complete, and score the exercise using available answer keys. Then go on to the Composition part of this guide.

Composition

This part of the guide will help you to create a new ending for one of the four short stories presented in this section. Follow the plan outlined on the next page.

Plan

- Begin with one of the following passages from the original story. Each passage appears at or near the point of greatest tension in the story.
- Change the events that follow the passage so that the outcome is different than in the original story.
- Write as if you are the author of the short story. Where applicable, include dialogue.

"The Boy Who Painted Christ Black"

> But for the monotonous lull of heavy breathing, I would have sworn that his words had frozen everyone in the hall. I had never heard the little principal speak so boldly to anyone, black or white.

"All the Years of Her Life"

> "You're a bad lot. God forgive you. It's one thing after another and always has been. Why do you stand there stupidly. Go to bed, why don't you?"

"Gaston"

> The man bought a kilo of peaches but found no flawed peaches among them, so he bought another kilo at another store, and this time there were two that were flawed. He hurried back to his flat and let himself in.

"The Monkey's Paw"

> But her husband was on his hands and knees groping wildly on the floor in search of the paw. If he could only find it before the thing outside got in.

Use the Checklist to help you review and revise your writing. Do this for all drafts and your final copy.

Checklist	**Yes**	**No**
1. I wrote a new ending for one of the four short stories I have read.	_____	_____
2. My new ending begins with a passage from the original story.	_____	_____
3. I changed the events that follow the passage so that the outcome is different than in the original story.	_____	_____
4. I wrote as if I were the author of the short story. Where appropriate, I included dialogue.	_____	_____
5. I used transitions to connect ideas and create unity in my writing.	_____	_____
6. I proofread and edited my composition.	_____	_____
7. I wrote a corrected copy of my work.	_____	_____

Submit the completed writing assignment and Practice exercise to your instructor for evaluation.

35.

Understanding Theme

This guide will help you to understand story themes. The theme of a story conveys the author's message about people and the world in which we live. One theme may be stated in different ways. One story may have several themes. The theme is expressed through all the elements of the short story.

Practice

Read each part of this exercise and answer all **21** questions. Passages from each of the four stories in this book appear on the following pages. In each, one of the three elements—setting, characterization, or conflict—is used to express the story's theme.

Identify the **dominant element** and **theme** of each passage. Write the element and indicate the theme by its appropriate letter. The first one is done for you.

Elements setting
characterization
conflict

from "The Boy Who Painted Christ Black"

Themes a. It is important to stand up for your beliefs.

b. Prejudice is a destructive force in our society.

The teacher always pronounced his name with profound gusto as she pointed him out as the ideal student. Once I heard her say: "If he were white he might, some day, become President." Only Aaron Crawford wasn't white; quite the contrary. His skin was so solid black that it glowed, reflecting an inner virtue that was strange, and beyond my comprehension.

1. **characterization**, **b**

For the teacher's birthday, which fell on a day about a week before commencement, Aaron Crawford painted the picture that caused an uproar, and a turning point, at the Muscogee County School.

2. ____________________, ______

The Muscogee County School for colored children.

3. ____________________, ______

On this day we were always favored with a visit from a man whom all the teachers spoke of with mixed esteem and fear. Professor Danual, they called him, and they always pronounced his name with reverence. He was supervisor of all the city schools, including those small and poorly equipped ones set aside for colored children.

4. ____________________, ______

"You are not being paid to teach such things in this school, and I am demanding your resignation for overstepping your limit as principal."

5. ____________________, ______

Elements setting
characterization
conflict

from "All the Years of Her Life"

Themes c. Growing up means taking responsibility for yourself.

d. Some parents sacrifice everything, including themselves, for their children.

Ever since Alfred had left school he had been getting into trouble wherever he worked.

6. ____________________, ______

They were closing the drugstore and getting ready to go home.

7. ____________________, ______

"He looks like a big fellow, doesn't he? It takes some of them a long time to get any sense," and they both stared at Alfred, who shifted away with a bit of light shining for a moment on his thin face and the tiny pimples over his cheekbone.

8. ____________________, ______

Without being alarmed, while being just large and still and simple and hopeful, she was becoming dominant there in the dimly lit store.

9. ____________________, ______

"Be quiet. Don't speak to me. You've disgraced me again and again," she said bitterly.

10. ____________________, ______

from "Gaston"

Themes e. Children are often pawns in adult relationships.

f. When you open your heart to others, you're open to hurt as well as love.

He was at home. She was with him in his home in Paris, if you could call it a home.

11. ____________________, ______

"Well, he used to live in this peach seed, but now that the peach has been harvested and sold, and I have eaten half of it, it looks as if he's out of house and home."

12. ____________________, ______

"Somebody else gets a peach with a bug in it, and throws it away, but not him. He makes up a lot of foolishness about it."

13. ____________________, ______

She cried a little, but only inside, because long ago she had decided she didn't like crying because if you ever started to cry it seemed as if there was so much to cry about you almost couldn't stop, and she didn't like that at all.

14. ____________________, ______

Elements setting
characterization
conflict

"Gaston" (continued)

He watched the huge car drive off, then he went around the corner where he took coffee every morning, feeling a little, he thought, like Gaston on the white plate.

15. ____________________, ______

from "The Monkey's Paw"

Themes g. If you interfere with fate, you'll be sorry.

h. We are all at the mercy of fate.

"It had a spell put on it by an old fakir," said the sergeant-major, "a very holy man. He wanted to show that fate ruled people's lives, and those who interfered with it did so to their sorrow."

16. ____________________, ______

At the third glass his eyes got brighter, and he began to talk, the little family circle regarding with eager interest this visitor from distant parts, as he squared his broad shoulders in the chair and spoke of strange scenes and doughty deeds, of wars and plagues and strange peoples.

17. ____________________, ______

"He was caught in the machinery," said the visitor at length, in a low voice.

18. ____________________, ______

Even his wife's face seemed changed as he entered the room. It was white and expectant, and to his fears seemed to have an unnatural look upon it. He was afraid of her.

19. ____________________, ______

"That's the worst of living so far out," bawled Mr. White, with sudden and unlooked-for violence; "of all the beastly, slushy, out-of-the-way places to live in, this is the worst. Pathway's a bog, and the road's a torrent."

20. ____________________, ______

Her husband was on his hands and knees groping wildly on the floor in search of the paw. If only he could find it before the thing outside got in.

21. ____________________, ______

Score the Practice exercise using the Answer Key, and go on to the Composition part of this guide.

Composition

This part of the guide will help you apply what you have learned about story themes. Write a three paragraph essay about the theme of **one** of the four stories presented in this section. Follow the outline below to write your essay.

Outline

I. The Introductory Paragraph

  A. State the title and author of the story.

  B. Tell where and when the story takes place.

  C. Briefly tell what the story is about.

II. The Development Paragraph

  A. Write a topic sentence that introduces the theme of the story.

  B. Find **two** passages in the story which convey the theme through setting, characterization, or conflict.

  C. For each, quote the passage and explain how it relates to the theme of the story.

  D. Write a concluding sentence which summarizes **this** paragraph.

III. The Concluding Paragraph

  A. What is the outcome of this story?

  B. How does the theme apply to people in general?

  C. How does the theme apply to you personally?

Use the Checklist to help you review and revise your writing. Do this for all drafts and your final copy.

Checklist	**Yes**	**No**
1. In my first paragraph I introduce the title and author, the setting, and tell what the story is about.	____	____
2. In the development paragraph I introduce the theme, quote two passages, and explain how each relates to the theme of the story.	____	____
3. In my concluding paragraph, I tell the outcome of the story. I also show how the theme applies to people in general, and to me personally.	____	____
4. I used transitions to connect ideas and create unity in my writing.	____	____
5. I proofread and edited my composition.	____	____
6. I wrote a corrected copy of my work.	____	____

Submit the completed writing assignment and Practice exercise to your instructor for evaluation.

36.

Point of View

This guide will help you to understand the purpose of point of view in a story. In life, the same event can be seen from different points of view, as illustrated in the cartoon. In a short story, **point of view refers to the position of the narrator and what he or she sees (interprets) from that vantage point.**

Basically, there are two positions from which a story can be told: first person and third person. A **first person narrator** is a character in the story. This narrator uses words like *I, me, my, we, our,* and *us.* "The Boy Who Painted Christ Black" is told from a first person point of view as illustrated by the following passage.

> Presently the Negro principal introduced the distinguished guest and he favored *us* with a short speech. It wasn't a very important speech. Almost at the end of it, *I* remember him saying something about he wouldn't be surprised if one of *us* boys grew up to be a great colored man, like Booker T. Washington.

A **third person narrator** is not a character in the story. This narrator uses words like *he, she, his, her,* and *they*. "Gaston" is told from the third person point of view, as illustrated by the following passage:

> *They* were to each peaches, as planned, after *her* nap, and now *she* sat across from the man who would have been a total stranger except that *he* was in fact *her* father.

Through point of view, the author tells us what is seen from the narrator's position. The author employs the narrator to introduce the setting, create characters, present conflicts and solutions, and develop themes. The author expresses attitudes, values, and opinions indirectly, through the narrator. A skillful author can make the reader experience what the narrator sees, feels, and believes. In effect, the author *talks* to the reader through the narrator.

Practice

Read each part of this exercise and answer all **37** questions. Presented below are passages from the four stories you have read in this section. Each passage is followed by three interpretations. Only one expresses the author's point of view. Select the **letter** of the phrase that best completes each statement.

from "The Boy Who Painted Christ Black"

1. ______ Truthfully, I could never make up my mind about him. Sometimes he looked like something out of a book of ancient history . . . looked as if he was left over from that magnificent era before the machine age came and marred the earth's natural beauty.

The narrator sees Aaron as an individual who appears:

a. ageless, rare, and magnificent.
b. comfortable with the age of technology.
c. to resemble a machine of some kind.

2. ______ Already the teacher sensed that Aaron had a present for her. Still smiling, he placed it on her desk and began to help her unwrap it. As the last piece of paper fell from the large frame, the teacher jerked her hand away from it suddenly, her eyes flickering unbelievingly. Amidst the rigid tension, her heavy breathing was distinct and frightening. Temporarily, there was no other sound in the room.

The words that **best** express the author's description of the teacher's reaction are:

a. hurt and resentment.
b. shock and disbelief.
c. annoyance and anger.

3. ______ When he rose to speak, to explain about the picture, a hush fell tightly over the room, and the children gave him all of their attention . . . something they rarely did for the teacher. He did not speak at first; he just stood there in front of the room, toying absently with his hands, observing his audience carefully, like a great concert artist.

The author is telling us that the other students in the class:

a. competed with Aaron for the teacher's attention.
b. ignored Aaron when he spoke.
c. respected and listened to Aaron.

4. ______ When I came close to the picture, I noticed it was painted with the kind of paint you get in the five and ten cent stores. Its shape was blurred slightly, as if someone had jarred the frame before the paint had time to dry. The eyes of Christ were deep-set and sad, very much like those of Aaron's father, who was a deacon in the local Baptist church. This picture of Christ looked much different from the one I saw hanging on the wall when I was in Sunday School. It looked more like a helpless Negro, pleading silently for mercy.

The point of view the narrator expresses here is designed to let the reader know:

a. the painting wasn't worth very much.
b. the painting was meant to be a vicious attack on another's beliefs.
c. the figure of Christ resembled people Aaron knew and loved.

5. ______ The great man arrived almost at the end of our commencement exercises. On seeing him enter the hall, the children rose, bowed courteously, and sat down again, their eyes examining him as if he were a circus freak.

From this information the reader can assume that:

a. Professor Danual frequently visited the school.
b. the students were not accustomed to having white people visit the school.
c. Professor Danual was deformed.

6. ______ "I painted it, sir." These were Aaron's words, spoken hesitantly. He wetted his lips timidly and looked up at the supervisor, his eyes voicing a sad plea for understanding.

Aaron's words and his behavior here fit that of a character who is:

a. elated.
b. annoyed.
c. scared.

7. ______ But for the monotonous lull of heavy breathing, I would have sworn that his words had frozen everyone in the hall. I had never heard the little principal speak so boldly to anyone, black or white.

The atmosphere in the hall at the moment is best described as:

a. excited and noisy.
b. shocked silence.
c. chilled and damp.

8. ______ The supervisor swallowed dumbfoundedly. His face was aglow in silent rage. "Have you been teaching these children things like that?"

"I have been teaching them that their race has produced great kings and queens as well as slaves and serfs," the principal said.

The principal responds to the supervisor's accusations by:

a. apologizing and hoping he will be forgiven.
b. stating his beliefs with pride and confidence.
c. blaming Aaron for causing so much trouble.

9. ______ The supervisor coughed. His eyes bulged menacingly as he spoke. "You are not being paid to teach such things in this school, and I am demanding your resignation for overstepping your limit as principal."

George Du Vaul did not speak. A strong quiver swept over his sullen face. He revolved himself slowly and walked away out of the room toward the office.

Through the conflict in this story, we see how racial prejudice:

a. forces George Du Vaul to choose between his job and his beliefs.
b. guarantees equality for all people.
c. protects Aaron's right to self-expression, learning, and achievement.

10. ______ An air of triumph gave more dignity to his soldierly stride. He had the appearance of a man who had done a great thing, something greater than any ordinary man would do. . . . Even from this distance I could see they were still walking in brisk, dignified strides, like two people who had won some sort of victory.

The author offers this description as a conclusion for the story. His main point is that:

a. the story has a happy ending.
b. at least Aaron and the principal have each other.
c. when you stand up for your convictions you may lose some things, but not your self respect.

from "All the Years of Her Life"

11. ______ He wanted to sound like a swaggering, big guy who could look after himself, yet the old, childish hope was in him, the longing that someone at home would come and help him.

The author is suggesting that when Alfred finds himself in trouble:

a. he must handle it alone.
b. it doesn't really bother him.
c. he relies on someone to rescue him.

12. ______ Mr. Carr was a little embarrassed by her lack of terror and her simplicity, and he hardly knew what to say to her, so she asked, "Is Alfred in trouble?"

The reader can infer from this passage that Mr. Carr was prepared to deal with someone who was:

a. less frightened than the mother.
b. more straightforward that the mother.
c. less composed than the mother.

13. ______ Alfred couldn't understand his mother's quiet composure, for if they had been at home and someone had suggested that he was going to be arrested, he knew she would be in a rage and cry out against him. Yet now she was standing there with that gentle, pleading smile on her face, saying, "I wonder if you don't think it would be better just to let him come home with me."

Through Alfred, the narrator is telling us that Mrs. Higgins:

a. expresses her true feelings.
b. puts up a good front.
c. is unable to cope with this situation.

14. ______ But even while he was turning away uneasily Alfred was realizing that Mr. Carr had become aware that his mother was really a fine woman; he knew that Sam Carr was puzzled by his mother, as if he had expected her to come in and plead with him tearfully, and instead he was being made to feel a bit ashamed by her vast tolerance.

The author makes us feel:

a. Alfred's admiration for his mother.
b. Alfred's fear of his mother.
c. Alfred's anger for his mother.

15. ______ "Of course, I don't want to be harsh," Mr. Carr was saying, "I'll tell you what I'll do. I'll just fire him and let it go at that. How's that?" and he got up and shook hands with Mrs. Higgins, bowing low to her in deep respect.

Mr. Carr has altered his point of view somewhat. He is now:

a. more upset than he was at the beginning of the story.
b. asking for Mrs. Higgins' approval of his decision.
c. sorry that he telephoned Mrs. Higgins.

16. ______ Alfred was afraid to speak to her, he was afraid of the silence that was between them, so he only looked ahead. . . . In a little while, going along like that in silence made him terribly aware of the strength and the sternness in her; he began to wonder what she was thinking of as she stared ahead so grimly.

The author is warning us that Mrs. Higgins' gentle manner in the drugstore was covering:

a. a forgiving attitude.
b. her total avoidance of the situation.
c. the anger she has been holding back up to this time.

17. ______ She said, "I'm going to make myself a cup of tea. Mind now, not a word about tonight to your father."

The author is telling the reader that in the Higgins family:

a. mother and father have equal responsibility for raising the children.
b. the mother is mainly responsible for raising the children.
c. the father is not concerned about his children.

18. ______ Her face, as she sat there, was a frightened, broken face utterly unlike the face of the woman who had been so assured a little while ago in the drugstore. . . . She looked very old. It seemed to Alfred that this was the way it had been every time he had been in trouble before, that this trembling had really been in her as she hurried out half dressed to the drugstore.

The narrator is telling us that the son realizes his mother:

a. appears strong to others, but is weak and worn on the inside.
b. has no effect on other people.
c. deserves the kind of life she is leading.

19. ______ He watched his mother, and he never spoke, but at that moment his youth seemed to be over; he knew all the years of her life by the way her hand trembled as she raised the cup to her lips. It seemed to him that this was the first time he had ever looked upon his mother.

In the end, Alfred appears to have made a decision to:

a. behave as he has in the past.
b. blame his mother for his troubles.
c. grow up and take responsibility for himself.

from "Gaston"

20. ______ The peach looked as good as the others, almost the size of a tennis ball, nice red fading to light green, but where the stem had been there was now <u>a break that went straight down into the heart of the seed</u>.

The meaning of these underlined words is made clear later on when:

a. the girl cries to herself and her father feels hurt when she leaves.
b. the phone rings and it is the mother.
c. Gaston wanders around on the plate.

21. ______ "Now, the poor fellow hasn't got a home, and there he is with all that pure design and handsome form, and nowhere to go. . . . Gaston is just about the handsomest of his kind I've ever seen."

By having the father give the bug a name and a history, the author is saying that:

a. adults often lie to children.
b. adults sometimes bore children with silly stories.
c. people have different viewpoints about bugs and lifestyles.

22. ______ "It's where he used to live. Gaston is out in the world and on his own now. You can see for yourself how comfortable he was in there. He had everything."
"Now what has he got?"
"Not very much, I'm afraid."

The father is talking about Gaston, but he may also be talking about:

a. himself.
b. the mother.
c. the girl.

23. ______ "Don't you want a peach?"
"Only if it's a peach with somebody in the seed."

The author is telling us, through the girl's response, that:

a. the girl like to play with bugs.
b. the girl supports her father's point of view of Gaston.
c. the girl is just trying to please her father.

24. ______ "If it's my mother, what shall I say?"
"Tell her I've gone to get you a bad peach, and anything else you want to tell her."

We know that the girl's parents do not live together. The author gives us a view of their present relationship through the father's choice of words and his tone which is basically:

a. gentle.
b. matter of fact.
c. sarcastic.

25. ______ "Let me speak to your father," she said.
"He's gone to get a peach."
"One peach?"
"One with people."
"You haven't been with your father two days and already you sound like him."
"There are peaches with people in them. I know. I saw one of them come out."
"A bug?"
"Not a bug. Gaston the grand something."
"Somebody else gets a peach with a bug in it, and throws it away, but not him. He makes up a lot of foolishness about it."

When the mother talks about the father, she:

a. discounts his point of view.
b. supports his efforts to communicate with his daughter.
c. compliments him.

26. ______ The girl watched Gaston on the plate, and she actually didn't like him. He was all *ugh,* as he had been in the first place. He didn't have a home anymore and he was wandering around on the white plate and he was silly and wrong and ridiculous and useless and all sorts of other things.

The feelings expressed in this passage reflect a change in the girl's point of view about Gaston and, therefore, about:

a. peaches.
b. her mother.
c. her father.

27. ______ "Where is Gaston?"
"I squashed him."
"Really? Why?"
"Everybody squashes bugs and worms."

The little girl is now expressing the same point of view as:

a. Gaston.
b. the mother.
c. the father.

28. ______ He watched the huge car drive off, then he went around the corner where he took coffee every morning, feeling a little, he thought, like Gaston on the white plate.

In this story, the author uses Gaston to help represent the feelings and situation of:

a. the father.
b. the girl.
c. the mother.

from "The Monkey's Paw"

29. ______ "That's the worst of living so far out," bawled Mr. White, with sudden and unlooked-for violence: "of all the beastly, slushy, out-of-the-way places to live in, this is the worst. Pathway's a bog, and the road's a torrent."

The narrator, in describing the surroundings with words like *sudden and unlooked-for violence* and *beastly* suggests that:

a. something fearful will occur.
b. Mr. White is thinking about moving.
c. Mr. White likes complaining about the weather.

30. ______ "The first man had his three wishes, yes," was the reply. "I don't know what the first two were, but the third was for death. That's how I got the paw."

The author, in telling this to the reader, is implying that:

a. the man's first two wishes were not granted.
b. the man was not happy with the results of the first two wishes.
c. the man was satisfied with the outcome of all three wishes.

31. ______ "If you keep it, don't blame me for what happens. Pitch it on the fire again, like a sensible man."

The sergeant-major, who has brought the paw back from India, advises Mr. White to:

a. make only frivolous wishes.
b. save the paw for an emergency.
c. get rid of the paw.

32. ______ Mr. White took the paw from his pocket and eyed it dubiously. "I don't know what to wish for, and that's a fact," he said slowly. "It seems to me I've got all I want."

If this is a man who has everything he wants, and it is said that the monkey's paw has caused mischief and sorrow, the author is trying to tell the reader:

a. we can always think of one more thing we'd like to have.
b. If you have everything you want, why tempt fate?
c. Mr. White is a confused man.

33. ______ "If you only cleared the house, you'd be quite happy, wouldn't you?" said Herbert, with his hand on his shoulder. "Well, wish for two hundred pounds, then; that'll just do it."

Through the character of Herbert the author is saying:

a. people are greedy.
b. people like to tell others what to do.
c. people unwittingly determine their own fate.

34. ______ They sat down by the fire again while the two men finished their pipes. Outside, the wind was higher than ever, and the old man started nervously at the sound of a door banging upstairs. A silence unusual and depressing settled upon all three, which lasted until the old couple rose to retire for the night.

Through the narrator, the author is creating a mood best expressed by these words:

a. quiet and comfortable.
b. agitated and worried.
c. busy and talkative.

35. ______ "I expect you'll find the cash tied up in a big bag in the middle of your bed," said Herbert, as he bade them good night, "and something horrible squatting up on top of the wardrobe watching you as you pocket your ill-gotten gains."

Often, the author will hint about a future occurrence in the story. This passage foretells of the point in the story when:

a. the man from Maw and Meggins brings the news about Herbert.
b. the old people return from the cemetery.
c. Herbert, all mangled, returns and is knocking at the door.

"We had the first wish granted," said the old woman feverishly; "why not the second?"
"A coincidence," stammered the old man.
"Go and get it and wish," cried the old woman, and dragged him toward the door.

36. ______ The husband has his point of view regarding the paw:

a. He has learned his lesson.
b. He is willing to tempt fate again.
c. He looks fondly upon the paw.

37. ______ The wife, on the other hand, holds a different point of view regarding the paw:

a. She has learned her lesson.
b. She is willing to tempt fate again.
c. She despises the paw.

Score the Practice exercise using the Answer Key, and go on to the Composition part of this guide.

Composition

This part of the guide will help you apply what you have learned about point of view. Choose **one** story from the four presented in this section. Tell the story from a new point of view, that of a first person narrator.

When you change the point of view in a story, different attitudes and feelings will be expressed. Use the outline presented to write your version of the story. **Write as if you are one of the following characters:**

- In "The Boy Who Painted Christ Black," you can write from the point of view of Aaron, the teacher, the principal, or the supervisor.
- In "All the Years of Her Life," you can write from the point of view of Alfred, Mrs. Higgins, or Sam Carr.
- In "Gaston," you can write from the point of view of the little girl, Gaston, the father, or the mother.
- In "The Monkey's Paw," you can write from the point of view of the sergeant-major, Mr. White, Herbert, Mrs. White, or the Paw (fate).

Outline

I. The Introductory Paragraph

  A. You are the first person narrator. This narrator uses words like *I, me, my, we, our,* and *us.*

  B. Introduce yourself and your role in the story.

  C. Tell where and when the story takes place. Include important background information.

  D. Introduce the main characters and their relationship to you.

II. The Development Paragraph

  A. Describe the conflict and your part in it. Refer to significant complications.

  B. Describe the climax and its effect on you.

  C. Describe the resolution of the conflict and how you feel about it.

III. The Concluding Paragraph

  A. Tell how the story ends.

  B. From your point of view, what is the theme of this story?

  C. Tell how you feel about the outcome of this story, and why?

Use the Checklist to help you review and revise your writing. Do this for all drafts and your final copy.

Checklist	**Yes**	**No**
1. I tell the story from a new point of view, as a first person narrator.	_____	_____
2. I describe the setting and include background information.	_____	_____
3. I introduce the main characters and describe their relationship to me.	_____	_____
4. I describe my role in the conflict, the climax, and the resolution.	_____	_____
5. I tell how the story ends, how I view the theme, and how I feel about the outcome.	_____	_____
6. I used transitions to connect ideas and create unity in my writing.	_____	_____
7. I proofread and edited my composition.	_____	_____
8. I wrote a corrected copy of my work.	_____	_____

Submit the completed writing assignment and Practice exercise to your instructor for evaluation.

37.

Creating a Short Story

This guide will help you to create your own short story. The other guides in this section about fiction have taught you the elements of the short story: setting, characterization, conflict and plot, theme, and point of view. This guide teaches you how to include these elements in your own short story.

Practice

Read each part of the following exercise and answer all **12** questions. This section of the guide is designed to help you create details and descriptions of characters and events for your story. Take time to think about your ideas before you begin to write. Your story may be based on an event or experience which illustrates some aspect of your life, or the lives of others. You may wish to write about real or imaginary events.

1. Write a title for your short story. You may prefer to create one after you have written the story.

   ____

2. Where does the story take place?

   ____

3. When does the story take place?

   ____

4. Provide some background information that is relevant to the story.

   ____

5. You may create one, two, three, or four characters for your story. For each, provide the following information.

   Name ______________________________

   Role in the story ______________________________

   Description ______________________________

6. Choose one character who will tell the story from a first person point of view.

   Character's name ______________________________

7. Make a list of the events that occur in the story, from beginning to end. This is your story line. Include at least four events in your list.

8. List the major conflict and complications that occur in the plot.

   Major conflict ______________________________

   Complications ______________________________

9. What is the point of greatest tension in the story?

   ____

10. How is the conflict resolved?

   ____

11. What happens to **each** of the characters at the end of the story?

   ____

12. What is the theme of the story, your message to the reader?

   ____

After you have completed the Practice exercise, go on to the composition part of this guide.

Composition

This part of the guide will help you to write your own short story. Use the material that you created in the Practice exercise to write your story. Follow the outline below.

Outline

I. Tell the story from a first person point of view. The narrator will be a character in the story.

II. Capture the reader's interest right at the beginning of the story. Here are some suggestions for how you can do this:

A. Open with a strong statement or ask a question.
B. Start with a detailed description of a person or a place.
C. Begin with a conversation between two characters.

III. Tell where and when the story takes place, and provide important background information. Offer significant details and descriptions. This helps to create atmosphere and enables the reader to *see* the people and places in your story.

IV. Make your characters come alive for the reader, both physically and emotionally. Reveal their personalities through the expression of thoughts, feelings, actions, and words.

V. Through the events in your story, present the conflict, complications, the climax, and the resolution.

VI. Reflect the theme through all the elements of your short story: setting, characterization, conflict and plot, and point of view.

Use the Checklist to help you review and revise your writing. Do this for all drafts and your final copy.

Checklist	Yes	No
1. My story has a first person narrator.	____	____
2. I capture the reader's interest at the beginning of the story.	____	____
3. I tell where and when the story takes place, provide background information, and create atmosphere by offering significant details and descriptions.	____	____
4. I make my characters real for the reader, both physically and emotionally.	____	____
5. Through the events in my story, I present the conflict, complications, the climax, and the resolution.	____	____
6. I reflect the theme through all the elements of my short story.	____	____
7. I used transitions to connect ideas and create unity in my writing.	____	____
8. I proofread and edited my short story.	____	____
9. I wrote a corrected copy of my work.	____	____

Submit the completed writing assignment and Practice exercise to your instructor for evaluation.

38.

The Book Report

This guide will help you to write a book report. The approach to writing a book report is similar to the one used to create your short story. Here, you will also be recording details and descriptions of characters and events. This time, however, the information will be based on the novel you have read.

Practice

This section of the guide is designed to help you collect and organize information for a book report. Read each part of the following exercise and answer all **13** questions.

1. Write the title of the book.

   ____

2. Write the author's name.

   ____

3. Write one or two sentences that tell what the book is about.

   ____

4. Who is the narrator of the story?

   ____

5. Where does the story take place?

   ____

6. When does the story take place?

   ____

7. Provide background information that is relevant to the story in the novel. ______________________________

8. Which of the five forms of conflict are presented in this novel? A novel, unlike a short story, will often have more than one form of conflict. ________________________

9. For each of the major characters in the novel (limit to four), give the following information:

   Name ______________________________________

   Character's role ______________________________

   Description __________________________________

10. Choose at least **two** scenes that express the major conflict and lead to further complications in the novel. Write the **page number** and the **sentence** that identifies the beginning of each scene.

    Page number __________

    Sentence ____________________________________

11. Choose a scene that involves the point of greatest tension. Write the **page number** and **sentence** that identifies the beginning of this scene.

    Page number __________

    Sentence ____________________________________

12. How does the novel end? _________________________

13. What is the author's message in the novel? ______________

After you have completed the Practice exercise, go on to the Composition part of this guide.

Composition

This part of the guide will help you to write a book report. Use the material that you have produced in the Practice exercise to write your report. Follow the outline presented here.

Outline

I. The Introductory Paragraph (**setting**)

  A. State the title and author of the book.

  B. Write one or two sentences that summarize what this book is about.

  C. Who is the narrator of the story?

  D. Where and when does the story take place? Provide relevant background information.

  E. Which of the five forms of conflict are presented in this novel?

II. Paragraphs Two through Five (**characterization**)

  A. Write a separate paragraph for each major character in the novel (limit to four). Develop each paragraph in the following way:

    1. Introduce the character by name and tell what role he or she plays in the story.

    2. Describe the character.

    3. What important interactions take place between this character and others in the story?

    4. What words spoken in the story help us to understand this character? Explain.

5. In what way, if any, does the character change by the end of the story?

6. How do you feel about this character, and why?

III. Paragraphs Six through Eight (**conflict and plot**)

A. Write a separate paragraph for each of three important scenes in the novel.

1. Describe **two** scenes that express the major conflict in the book, and show how they lead to further complications.

2. Describe **the scene** that involves the point of greatest tension in the story, and show how it leads to the resolution of the conflict.

IV. Paragraph Nine (**theme**)

A. Tell how the novel ends.

B. What is the author's message?

C. How does the theme apply to people in general?

D. How does the theme apply to you personally?

V. Paragraph Ten (**your opinion**)

A. Tell whether or not you liked this book, and why.

B. How did the book reinforce, or change, any attitudes or opinions you may have had?

C. Would you recommend this book to others? Why or why not?

Use the Checklist to help you review and revise your writing. Do this for all drafts and your final copy.

Checklist	**Yes**	**No**
1. In my introductory paragraph I state the title and author, summarize the story, and indicate the narrator. I describe the setting and the form(s) of conflict presented in this novel.	____	____
2. Paragraphs two through five each describe a major character in the novel, according to the outline.	____	____
3. Paragraphs six and seven describe scenes that express the major conflict in the book.	____	____
4. Paragraph eight describes a scene that involves the point of greatest tension in the novel.	____	____
5. In paragraph nine, I tell how the novel ends and the author's message. I show how the theme applies to people in general and to me personally.	____	____
6. In paragraph ten, I tell how I feel about the book.	____	____
7. I used transitions to connect ideas and create unity in my writing.	____	____
8. I proofread and edited my report.	____	____
9. I wrote a corrected copy of my work.	____	____

Submit the completed writing assignment and Practice exercise to your instructor for evaluation.

Picasso
You're the Best

IV.

Letters and Reports

Letter and report writing are often required on the job, in school, and in your personal life. A letter may be used as an introduction when applying for a job or requesting an interview. A cover letter is almost always included when sending a resume. People often write letters to order by mail, as well as to complain when they don't get what they ordered.

The persuasive essay can take the form of a letter or a report. In each, your purpose is to influence the reader to see things your way. The short report and the research paper are used to present facts in an organized and informative manner. This section ends with Writing Appraisal II, which will help you measure your progress in this course.

Guides

Preparing a Resume
Business Letter: Employment
Business Letter: Ordering
Business Letter: Complaint
The Persuasive Essay
The Short Report
The Research Paper
Writing Appraisal II

39.

Preparing a Resume

This guide will help you to write a resume. A clearly written resume can be a real advantage when you are looking for a job. The primary purpose of a resume is to get you an interview. A resume summarizes information about your life experiences and conveys a picture of you as a person. By preparing a resume, you show a prospective employer that you want to make a good first impression.

There are many ways to use your resume, as the following list illustrates:

- answering ads
- sending it to organizations where you seek employment
- distributing it to friends, family, or other acquaintances for networking
- giving it to a person writing a letter of reference for you
- attaching it to a job application

Practice

Read the sample resume, then complete the exercise that follows. This part of the guide will help to organize the data necessary to write your own resume.

RESUME

Renee Osborne
25 West 98th Street, New York, NY 10071 (212) 315-8022

Career Goal

I am interested in challenging work with children as a teacher and counselor.

Work Experience

Counselor —	YMCA Day Camp, New York, NY
6/98–8/98	Supervised and coordinated activities of handicapped girls, ages 10-12.
Volunteer —	West End Day Care Center, New York, NY
6/97–8/97	Supervised games and activities of youngsters, ages 2-4.

Education

9/98—	City College of New York, New York, NY
9/94–6/98	Louis D. Brandeis High School, New York, NY Regents Diploma

Special Skills

Typing, American sign language, piano

Interests and Hobbies

Swimming, music, running, photography

Awards and Achievements

Honor Society, Service Award, Lifesaving Certificate

References

Ms. Valerie Fernandez
Director, YMCA Day Camp
2010 Richmond Street
New York, NY 10002

Dr. James Palmer
Department of Psychology
City College of New York
New York, NY 10034

Once you provide all of the information requested below, you will be ready to write your own resume.

Identification Heading

This information is presented at the top of the page.

1. Your name ______________________________

2. Street address ______________________________

3. City, state, and zip code ______________________________

4. Telephone number (   ) ______________________________

Career Goal

What do you want to be? Express your long-range career goals in terms of the education you wish to attain and/or the work you want to do.

5. ______________________________

In the sample resume, WORK EXPERIENCE is presented first, followed by EDUCATION. The order of these categories is interchangeable; the one you wish to emphasize comes first. In either case, your most **recent** accomplishment is listed **first.** Other experiences follow in reverse order, from present to past.

Work Experience

How many jobs will you be listing on your resume? If you've had many jobs, list those you've held the longest and those that are most relevant to the work you are now seeking. You may have received pay for some, and volunteered your services at others. For each position, provide the data as requested in items 6-10 below. Your most recent job is listed first.

6. Job title: ______________________________

7. Name of employer (agency or company):

____

8. Location of employment (city and state only):

____

9. Job responsibilities (complete sentences not necessary):

____

10. Dates of employment (give month and year you began work, and month and year the job ended):

______________ to ______________

Education

List the secondary and postsecondary schools you have attended: high school, college, career institute, etc. Begin with your most recent experience and work backwards.

11. Name of school ______________________________

12. Location (city and state) ______________________________

13. Degree granted ______________________________

14. Dates attended (month and year) __________ to __________

The next three categories pertain to your skills, interests, hobbies, and special achievements. You may have data to include for all three categories, just two categories, or only one. If you have no data for a category, eliminate that category from your resume.

Special Skills

A skill is an ability in which you have demonstrated competence. You can do it well. For example, a measure of typing skill is expressed by the number of words you can type, per minute, without error.

There are other skills in which competence is measured by a successful outcome. The ability to maintain or repair the engine so that your car runs well is a valuable skill to have.

15. List your skills:

____

Interests and Hobbies

An interest is something that holds our attention over a period of time. We become actively involved with an interest or hobby because the activity is rewarding. Some examples are: swimming, basketball, dancing, music, photography, and drawing.

When you develop competence in an interest, you have acquired a new skill. When you start swimming competitively on a team, your hobby is now a skill. When your musical ability leads you to performing with a band on weekends, your interest has become a skill.

16. List your interests and hobbies:

____

Awards and Achievements

17. List awards, honors, certificates, and other formal recognition of your accomplishments:

____

References

A prospective employer may want to contact people who know you and can provide a reference. Employers usually ask for information which includes:

- verification of your education and work experience.
- previous job evaluations.
- assessment of your character.

It is to your advantage to have positive references. Before you list someone, ask that person directly if they would agree to provide a reference for you. Do ask: teachers, guidance counselors, previous employers, neighbors, your physician, or minister. References from relatives are not recommended. List at least **two** references.

18. Name of reference ________________________________

    Agency or company (if applicable):

    ____

    Address of reference (business or residence):

    ____

    City, state and zip code:

    ____

Once you have completed the Practice exercise, go on to the Composition part of this guide.

Composition

In this part of the guide you will be writing your own resume. Refer to the model as you present your information. Type the final copy of your resume on unlined bond paper.

Use the Checklist to help you review and revise your writing. Do this for all drafts and your final copy.

Checklist	Yes	No
1. I used information I provided in the Practice exercise to write my resume.	_____	_____
2. I followed the format of the sample resume.	_____	_____
3. The Identification Heading is at the top of the page.	_____	_____
4. My work and educational experiences are listed in reverse chronological order, from present to past.	_____	_____
5. I included special skills, interests, and awards where relevant.	_____	_____
6. I proofread and edited my resume.	_____	_____
7. I typed the final copy of my resume on unlined bond paper.	_____	_____

Submit the completed writing assignment and Practice exercise to your instructor for evaluation.

40.

Business Letter: Employment

This guide will help you to write a business letter. The focus of your writing will be a letter of application for a job. In it, you can introduce yourself and request an interview. This letter accompanies your resume when writing to a prospective employer.

Cover letters use the business letter format, as shown in the model. The six parts of the letter are labeled as follows:

HEADING

INSIDE ADDRESS

GREETING

BODY

CLOSING

SIGNATURE

Practice

Read each part of the following exercise and answer all **24** questions. Begin with the model cover letter on the next page.

Heading

25 West 98th Street
New York, NY 10071
September 15, 1998

Ms. Martha Robbins
The New Day Residence
P.O. Box 2047
Brooklyn, NY 12249

Inside Address

Dear Ms. Robbins:

Greeting

Body

I am writing to apply for the position of part-time Resident Assistant which was listed with the Career Placement Office at City College.

I worked with handicapped children in a previous job at the YMCA Day Camp. I found this experience very rewarding. I was also a volunteer at a day care center. I like working with youngsters and plan to make a career of teaching and counseling children.

I have enclosed a resume which summarizes my experiences and qualifications. I would like to have the opportunity to discuss this position in a personal interview, and would be pleased to meet you at your convenience. I can be reached evenings at (212) 315-8022.

Closing — Sincerely,

Signature — Renee Osborne

Renee Osborne

Enc.

For the following exercise, write the **letter** of the phrase that best completes each sentence.

1. ______ The address in the **heading** belongs to the person:

   a. writing the letter.

   b. reading the letter.

2. ______ The **inside address** belongs to the person:

   a. writing the letter.

   b. receiving the letter.

3. ______ The **greeting** is directed at the person:

   a. writing the letter.

   b. receiving the letter.

4. ______ The **body** of the letter gives information about the person:

   a. writing the letter.

   b. receiving the letter.

5. ______ The **closing** of the business letter is sincere, yet formal. Which of the following would *not* be an appropriate closing?

   a. Yours truly,

   b. Respectfully,

   c. Sincerely,

   d. Your friend,

6. ______ The writer's **signature** appears:

a. in the heading.

b. after the closing.

The following list includes the kind of information presented in the model letter. This information can be grouped and ordered into three paragraphs: introduction, middle, and conclusion. For each phrase, write the letter *A* if the information appears in the first paragraph, *B* if it appears in the second paragraph, or *C* if it appears in the third paragraph.

7. ______ reference to enclosed resume
8. ______ the position applied for
9. ______ relevant career goals
10. ______ why you are writing
11. ______ request for an interview
12. ______ reasons for wanting this job
13. ______ how you heard of the opening
14. ______ how you can be reached
15. ______ qualifications to do this work

Now that you have grouped this information by paragraph, write each phrase in the appropriate order according to the outline below.

A. Introductory Paragraph

16. ________________________________

17. ________________________________

18. ________________________________

B. **Middle Paragraph**

19. ______________________________

20. ______________________________

21. ______________________________

C. **Concluding Paragraph**

22. ______________________________

23. ______________________________

24. ______________________________

Score the Practice exercise using the Answer Key, and go on to the Composition part of this guide.

Composition

This part of the guide will help you to apply what you have learned about writing a business letter. Write a letter in which you introduce yourself and request a job interview. On the next page is a list of six job openings. You may write to any one of these, or respond to an actual job advertisement. Use the outline on page 272. Type or write the final copy of your letter.

Job Openings

Part-time road worker
Ace Asphalt Paving Company
6300 South Dixie Highway
Jacksonville, Florida 32250

Punch key operator—will train
Evenings and weekends
Computer Data Systems
800 Delaware Avenue
Cleveland, Ohio 44108

Salesclerk—flexible hours, good benefits
Gap Stores, Inc.
8323 W. Spruce Street
Dallas, Texas 75281

Food concession—weekends and summer season
Taco Don's Inc.
One Towers Drive
Los Angeles, California 90011

Part-time receptionist
Maxim's Beauty Salon
2049 Century Park
Atlanta, Georgia 30309

Guided Tours, Inc.
1011 West Washington Street
Chicago, Illinois 60607

Follow the business letter format. Use *Dear Sir or Madam:* as your greeting if the name of the person doing the hiring is not known. Follow the outline below and refer to the model in the Practice exercise as you write your letter.

Outline

I. Introductory Paragraph

  A. Tell why you are writing.

  B. State the position applied for.

  C. Indicate how you heard of the opening.

II. Middle Paragraph

  A. Give your qualifications for this work.

  B. State your reasons for wanting this job.

  C. Refer to your relevant career goals.

III. Concluding Paragraph

  A. Refer to the enclosed resume.

  B. Request a personal interview.

  C. Tell how you can be reached.

Below the signature of your letter, at the left margin, you may want to include additional information such as *Enc.* (something is enclosed with the letter), or *cc: Jack Butler* (a carbon copy is being sent to the person named).

The envelope for the letter should show your name and address in the upper left corner and the addressee's name, title, and address in the center.

Use the Checklist to help you review and revise your writing. Do this for all drafts and your final copy.

Checklist	**Yes**	**No**
1. I wrote a letter of application introducing myself and requesting a job interview.	_____	_____
2. I used the business letter format as presented in the model.	_____	_____
3. The body of my letter contains three paragraphs. I explain why I am writing, give my qualifications, my reasons for wanting the job, and request an interview.	_____	_____
4. I used transitions to connect ideas and create unity in my writing.	_____	_____
5. I proofread and edited my business letter.	_____	_____
6. I typed or wrote a corrected copy of my work.	_____	_____

Submit the completed writing assignment and Practice exercise to your instructor for evaluation.

41.

Business Letter: Ordering

This guide will help you to understand how to order merchandise by letter. The business letter format is always the same, regardless of your purpose; however, the kind of information that goes into the body of the letter will change.

Practice

Read each part of the following exercise and answer all **38** questions. Begin with the model letter on the next page in which Ben Franklin orders a kite.

Heading

823 Stonybrook Road
Philadelphia, PA 19132
July 7, 1998

Fly by Night Novelties
2468 Adventure Avenue
San Francisco, CA 90083

Inside Address

Dear Sir or Madam:

Greeting

Body

I would like to order one blue silk kite, model number K3. Please print the following words on the kite in day-glo orange, at no extra charge:

YOU'RE THE BEST!

I have enclosed a check for $10 to cover the cost of the kite, plus postage and handling. Please send this order via "Speedy Service" as advertised.

Closing Sincerely,

Signature Ben Franklin

Ben Franklin

Enc.

Select words from the list to fill in the blanks below. Refer to the model letter to help you complete this exercise. Some words will be used more than once.

name	day	two	: (colon)
year	zip code	state	street address
body	cities	closing	capital letters
sent	explains	date	Dear Sir or Madam
sign	greeting	product	inside address
cost	comma	signature	lower case letter

The Heading Questions 1-8 refer to the heading of the letter.

1. The first line of the heading is the ______________ of the person who is writing the letter.
2. The second line of the heading contains the city, ______________, and zip code.
3. Names of streets, cities, and states always begin with ______________.
4. There is always a ______________ after the name of the city.
5. The ______________ appears after the name of the state.
6. The ______________ always appears on the third line of the heading.
7. The date includes the month, the day, and the ______________.
8. A comma is placed between the ______________ and the year.

The Inside Address Questions 9-12 refer to the inside address of the letter.

9. Skip at least two lines after the heading and begin the ______________.

10. The ______________ of the company is the first line of the inside address. (If you are writing to a specific individual, that name will appear on the first line. The company name will appear on the second line.)

11. Names of streets, ______________, and states begin with capital letters.

12. The zip code appears after the name of the ______________.

The Greeting Questions 13-15 refer to the greeting of the letter.

13. Skip three lines after the inside address and write the ______________.

14. Unless you have an individual's name, use the words ______________ as your greeting.

15. The greeting always ends with a ______________.

The Body Questions 16-21 refer to the body of the letter.

16. Skip three lines after the greeting and begin the ______________ of the letter.

17. The body is the part of the letter which ______________ why you are writing.

18. The body of this letter contains ______________ paragraphs.

19. The first paragraph contains specific information relating to the ______________ that is being ordered.

20. The second paragraph contains information about the ______________ of the product and where it is to be

21. ______________.

The Closing Questions 22-24 refer to the closing of the letter.

22. Skip three lines after the body of the letter and write the ________________.

23. Closings such as *Sincerely, Sincerely yours,* and *Yours truly,* are always followed by a ________________.

24. When a closing has two words, such as *Sincerely yours,* or *Yours truly,* the second word begins with a ________________.

The Signature Questions 25-26 refer to the signature of the letter.

25. Skip five lines after the closing and type or print your full name. This insures that the reader will know the spelling of your name. ________________ your name in the space between the closing and your typed or printed name.

26. Both your signed name and your typed or printed name are referred to as the ________________.

The following list includes the kind of information provided in the model letter. This information can be grouped and ordered into two paragraphs. For each phrase, write the letter *A* if the information appears in the first paragraph, or *B* if it appears in the second paragraph.

27. ______ how you plan to pay for merchandise (check, credit card, money order, C.O.D.)

28. ______ special instructions, if any (color, size, inscription)

29. ______ brief description of product, including model or reference number (if given)

30. ______ indicate the product you are ordering

31. ______ reference to postage and handling

32. ______ how you would like product shipped (if there is a choice)

Now that you have grouped the information by paragraphs, write each phrase in the appropriate order according to the outline below.

A. Opening Paragraph

33. ______________________________

34. ______________________________

35. ______________________________

B. Closing Paragraph

36. ______________________________

37. ______________________________

38. ______________________________

Score the Practice exercise using the Answer Key, and go on to the Composition part of this guide.

Composition

This part of the guide will help you to apply what you have learned about ordering merchandise by letter. Respond to one of the following advertisements. Ads like these appear regularly in newspapers and magazines. Use the outline presented to help you write your letter. Type or write the final copy of your letter.

Advertisements

AMAZING JEWELRY OFFER! 14 karat gold chains—16″, 18″, 20″. Chains incredibly priced at $49.95, $59.95, and $69.95. Please specify size. Add $2.50 for postage, handling, and insurance. Send check or money order to: Marvelous Metals, Inc., 3034 Woodward Avenue, Detroit, Michigan 48271.

SUPER SHIRT SPECIAL! 100% cotton T-shirts in your choice of color. $6 each! Up to six words printed free. Write desired inscription in block letters. Specify shirt **color:** red, blue, yellow, black, or white and **size:** small, medium, large, Xlarge. Add $1.95 for shipping and handling. Allow six weeks for delivery. For *rush* service, include additional $1.00. Send check, money order, or credit card number to: Shirt Special, P.O. Box 1950, Houston, Texas 77053.

PARTY FAVORS! Order unique party favors by mail at discount prices! Guaranteed to keep your friends laughing. Assorted balloon figures—politicians, movie stars, and cartoon characters—$7.95 per hundred; offbeat noisemakers, ten for $7.50; set of magic tricks, $5.95. Add 10% for postage and handling. Send check or money order to: Fantasy Fun, Inc., P.O. Box 31, Denver, Colorado 80215

Outline

I. Opening Paragraph

  A. State the product you are ordering.

  B. Give a brief description of product, including model or reference number (if given).

C. Provide special instructions, such as color, size, or inscription.

II. Closing Paragraph

A. Tell how you plan to pay for merchandise (check, credit card, money order, C.O.D.)

B. Make reference to payment for postage and handling.

C. State how you would like product shipped, if there is a choice.

Use the Checklist to help you review and revise your writing. Do this for all drafts and your final copy.

Checklist	Yes	No
1. I wrote a letter in which I ordered merchandise.	_____	_____
2. I used the business letter format.	_____	_____
3. The body of my letter contains two paragraphs. I describe the product, include special instructions, and make payment and shipping arrangements.	_____	_____
4. I used transitions to connect ideas and create unity in my writing.	_____	_____
5. I proofread and edited my business letter.	_____	_____
6. I typed or wrote the final copy of my work.	_____	_____

Submit the completed writing assignment and Practice exercise to your instructor for evaluation.

42.

Business Letter: Complaint

This guide will help you to understand how to write a letter of complaint. When you are dissatisfied with a product or a service, you may want to register a complaint with the seller in a formal way. You are more likely to get a response and quick resolution to the problem if you put it in writing.

Practice

Read each part of the following exercise and answer all **12** questions.

On July 4th, Benjamin Franklin ordered a blue silk kite, model number K3. The words, "YOU'RE THE BEST!" were to be inscribed in day-glo orange. The cost of the kite, plus postage and handling, was ten dollars.

On July 20th, he received the kite with the words, "YOU'RE THE BEAST!" written in bright orange on the material. The letter of complaint he wrote about this problem appears on the next page.

823 Stonybrook Road
Philadelphia, PA 19132
July 22, 1998

Fly by Night Novelties
2468 Adventure Avenue
San Francisco, CA 90083

Dear Sir or Madam:

On July 4, 1998, I ordered a blue silk kite, model number K3. I asked that the words "YOU'RE THE BEST!" be inscribed in day-glo orange. I sent you a check for ten dollars to cover the cost of the kite, plus postage and handling.

On July 20th, I received the kite as ordered, with the words "YOU'RE THE BEAST!" written in bright orange. The kite is fine, but I don't think the inscription is suitable as a gift the way it is. I am returning the kite and ask that you send me a new one, with the words "YOU'RE THE BEST!" written on it. Please rush this so I can have it by August 8th, in time for my wife's birthday.

Sincerely,

Ben Franklin

The following list includes the kind of information presented in the model letter of complaint. This information can be grouped and ordered into two paragraphs. For each phrase, write the letter *A* if the information appears in the first paragraph, or the letter *B* if it appears in the second paragraph.

1. ______ cost of product, including shipping
2. ______ date you received product
3. ______ what you want the seller to do
4. ______ description of product received, including defects
5. ______ date you ordered product
6. ______ detailed description of product ordered, including model number

Now that you have grouped the information by paragraph, write each phrase in the appropriate order according to the outline below.

Outline

A. Opening Paragraph

7. ______________________________
8. ______________________________
9. ______________________________

B. Closing Paragraph

10. ______________________________
11. ______________________________
12. ______________________________

Score the Practice exercise using Answer Key, and go on to the Composition part of this guide.

Composition

This part of the guide will help you to apply what you have learned about writing a letter of complaint. In the last guide, you responded to one of several advertisements by ordering a product. Below is a list of problems which occurred with each of the products ordered. Write a letter of complaint about the product that you ordered using the information and the outline provided. Type or write the final copy of your letter.

Problems

- The 14 karat gold chain you ordered turned out to be gold filled (dipped in gold, but not solid).
- The 100% cotton T-shirt you ordered for yourself shrank to half its size in the first washing.
- You ordered all three party favors advertised. You received the magic tricks and the noisemakers, but not the balloons.

Outline

I. Opening Paragraph

   A. Identify the product and give the date it was ordered.

   B. Provide a detailed description of product ordered, including model number.

   C. Indicate the cost of the product; include shipping charges.

II. Closing Paragraph

A. Give the date you received product.

B. Describe the product received, including defects.

C. State what you want the seller to do about this problem.

Use the Checklist to help you review and revise your writing. Do this for all drafts and your final copy.

Checklist	**Yes**	**No**
1. I wrote a letter of complaint about my order to the seller.	____	____
2. I used the business letter format.	____	____
3. The body of my letter contains two paragraphs. The first paragraph tells what I ordered. The second paragraph tells what I received and what I want the seller to do.	____	____
4. I used transitions to connect ideas and create unity in my writing.	____	____
5. I proofread and edited my business letter.	____	____
6. I typed or wrote the final copy of my work.	____	____

Submit the completed writing assignment and Practice exercise to your instructor for evaluation.

43.

The Persuasive Essay: A

This guide will help you to understand how a persuasive essay is written. Persuasive writing appeals to your ability to reason and to your emotions. This approach attempts to make the reader think, feel, and even act in a certain way. Persuasion is usually successful when the writer provides good reasons for doing, or not doing, something. Writing persuasively will convince the reader to see things **your** way.

In writing a persuasive essay, it is important to identify four elements of the situation you are writing about. These elements are defined here by the acronym, *PASS*.

Purpose—why you are writing

Audience—to whom you are writing

Subject—the topic of the essay

Status of writer—who you are

Persuasive writing can take the form of an essay, a letter, or a memorandum (memo). **The same content can be presented in any of these forms; only the headings change.** The heading of an essay tells you its title and author. Essay form is most often used by students. The business letter format is used to write a formal message. The memo is used when communicating within the same organization. The memo is less formal than the letter, and conveys less information in the heading. The memo assumes that people know one another.

Practice

Read each part of the following exercise and answer all **15** questions. The model essay takes the form of a memo. The author, an employee of the firm, attempts to convince the Director of Personnel to implement a stress management program for company employees. He does this by offering reasons why such a program would be beneficial to all.

October 24, 1998

To: Maria Arias,
Director of Personnel

From: Jim Kennedy,
Sales Manager

Subject: Stress management program for employees

As an employee of this company, I would like to suggest that the Personnel Department offer a program in stress management. Many corporations offer this training to their workers as a means of improving productivity and reducing absenteeism. I believe such a program would benefit our company and its employees.

If our company were to implement a stress management program, I am certain one result would be greater productivity. One out of every five of the Fortune 500 companies now have some kind of stress management program. Many firms realize that too much stress makes workers inefficient. Pressure improves performance to a point, after which efficiency drops off sharply. Learning how to relax and manage stress can actually improve the productivity of employees.

Linked to the need to improve performance and productivity is the need to reduce absenteeism and medical costs. Stress is known to be a major contributor, either directly or indirectly, to heart disease, cancer, lung ailments, accidents, and suicide. By encouraging workers to reduce the strain on their bodies and minds, some companies have been able to make significant reductions in the incidence of stress-related diseases among their employees. Stress management has led to lower medical costs and fewer work hours lost due to absenteeism.

Stress management programs are very popular because they make good business sense. Our firm can have healthier, happier, more productive employees and higher profits. I hope that your department will consider my suggestion and implement a program to combat stress.

Use the model essay to answer the questions below.

The Introductory Paragraph

1. Write a sentence that states the author's purpose.

   ____

2. The writer's audience is:

   ____

3. Indicate the subject of the essay.

   ____

4. Refer to the status of the writer.

   ____

5. What **two** reasons does the author give in support of his suggestion?

   ____

6. Write the sentence that expresses the author's opinion.

   ____

Development Paragraph One

In a persuasive essay, **each** development paragraph explains **one reason** for the author's opinion.

7. Write the topic sentence that states the first reason in support of the author's opinion.

   ____

8. Write the **number** of sentences which help to explain this first reason. ______________

9. Write the sentence which restates the topic and concludes this paragraph.

____

Development Paragraph Two

10. Write the topic sentence that states the second reason in support of the author's opinion.

____

11. Write the **number** of sentences which help to explain the second reason. ______________

12. Write the sentence which restates the topic and concludes this paragraph.

____

The Concluding Paragraph

13. Write the sentence that restates the topic of the essay.

____

14. Write a sentence that supports this restatement.

____

15. Write the sentence that summarizes the author's opinion and concludes the essay.

____

Score the Practice exercise using the Answer Key, and go on to the Composition part of this guide.

Composition

This part of the guide will help you to write a persuasive essay. Respond to **one** of the four situations presented below with a persuasive composition. You may choose to write this as an essay or a memo. Follow the outline on the next page as you write.

Situations

1.	Purpose:	To persuade your legislator to vote for or against a law which prohibits smoking in the dining area of restaurants.
	Audience:	Your legislator.
	Subject:	Smoking in the dining area of restaurants.
	Status of writer:	Identify yourself as the writer.
2.	Purpose:	As a member of the local Board of Education, persuade your colleagues to your position regarding sex education in the schools.
	Audience:	Your local Board of Education.
	Subject:	Sex education in the schools.
	Status of writer:	Identify yourself as the writer.
3.	Purpose:	To persuade a friend, relative, or colleague to lend you one thousand dollars.
	Audience:	A specific individual.
	Subject:	A $1,000 loan.
	Status of writer:	Identify yourself as the writer.

4. Purpose: To persuade readers of a newspaper or magazine to your point of view regarding the death penalty (Letters to the Editor).

   Audience: Readers of a newspaper or magazine.

   Subject: The death penalty.

   Status of writer: Identify yourself as the writer.

Outline

I. The Introductory Paragraph

   A. In your opening sentence(s), introduce your purpose, audience, subject, and your status as writer. This information can be presented in any order.

   B. State two reasons that support your persuasive argument, but do not explain them here.

   C. Express your opinion and conclude the paragraph.

II. Development Paragraph One

   A. Write a topic sentence that states the first reason in support of your argument.

   B. Write several sentences which explain this reason. Be specific and use details.

   C. Restate the topic of this paragraph and write a conclusion.

III. Development Paragraph Two

   A. Write a topic sentence that states the second reason in support of your argument.

   B. Write several sentences which explain this reason. Be specific and use details.

   C. Restate the topic of this paragraph and write a conclusion.

IV. The Concluding Paragraph

   A. Restate the subject of the essay.

   B. Support this restatement in a sentence or two.

   C. Summarize your opinion and conclude the essay.

Use the Checklist to help you review and revise your writing. Do this for all drafts and your final copy.

Checklist	**Yes**	**No**
1. In my opening sentence(s) I introduce my purpose, audience, subject, and my status as writer (PASS).	____	____
2. In my first paragraph, I state two reasons that support my argument. I express my opinion and conclude the paragraph.	____	____
3. Each of my development paragraphs introduce and explain one reason in support of my argument.	____	____
4. In my concluding paragraph I restate the subject of the essay, support it, express my opinion, and conclude the essay.	____	____
5. I used transitions to connect ideas and create unity in my writing.	____	____
6. I proofread and edited my composition.	____	____
7. I wrote a corrected copy of my work.	____	____

Submit the completed writing assignment and Practice exercise to your instructor for evaluation.

44.

The Persuasive Essay: B

The first part of this guide gives you an opportunity to practice your grammar, usage, and punctuation. It can also be used to improve your spelling, learn new words, and sharpen your reading comprehension skills. These activities will help to improve your writing.

Skills Practice

Choose one or more of the following exercises and answer at least **thirty** questions:

A **corrective** exercise recommended by your instructor.

A **spelling** exercise from available materials.

A **vocabulary** exercise from available materials.

A **reading comprehension** exercise from available materials.

Record the number of questions you complete, and score the exercise using available answer keys. Then go on to the Composition part of this guide.

Composition

This section of the guide provides additional practice in writing a persuasive essay. Resumes and business letters present facts in an effort to indirectly persuade the reader. The persuasive essay, on the other hand, attempts to influence the reader directly with facts as well as opinions.

Persuasion is often used in writing to the editor of a newspaper or magazine, and in contacting school, college, or public officials. It can also be effective in personal communication with a friend, relative, colleague, or supervisor. In many occupations, the ability to write persuasively can be a major asset. Persuasion is the primary focus of writing in the advertising industry.

Write a persuasive essay for **one** of the four situations presented here. Use the outline provided to do this. Before you write, identify the four elements of your situation: **P**urpose, **A**udience, **S**ubject, and **S**tatus of writer.

Situations

- Write a letter to the editor of a newspaper or magazine about an issue of your choice.
- Write a letter to a school, college, or public official making a request, or offering your opinion about an issue.
- Write an advertisement in the form of a persuasive essay for a product you are selling.
- Write a personal letter of persuasion to a friend, relative, colleague, or supervisor.

Outline

I. The Introductory Paragraph

A. In your opening sentence(s) introduce your purpose, audience, subject, and your status as writer. This information can be presented in any order.

B. State two reasons that support your persuasive argument, but do not explain them here.

C. Express your opinion and conclude the paragraph.

II. Development Paragraph One

A. Write a topic sentence that states the first reason in support of your argument.

B. Write several sentences which explain this reason. Be specific and use details.

C. Restate the topic of this paragraph and write a conclusion.

III. Development Paragraph Two

A. Write a topic sentence that states the second reason in support of your argument.

B. Write several sentences which explain this reason. Be specific and use details.

C. Restate the topic of this paragraph and write a conclusion.

IV. The Concluding Paragraph

A. Restate the subject of the essay.

B. Support this restatement in a sentence or two.

C. Summarize your opinion and conclude the essay.

Use the Checklist to help you review and revise your writing. Do this for all drafts and your final copy.

Checklist	**Yes**	**No**
1. In my opening sentence(s) I introduce my purpose, audience, subject, and my status as writer (PASS).	_____	_____
2. In my first paragraph, I state two reasons that support my argument. I express my opinion and conclude the paragraph.	_____	_____
3. Each of my development paragraphs introduce and explain one reason in support of my argument.	_____	_____
4. In my concluding paragraph I restate the subject of the essay, support it, express my opinion, and conclude the essay.	_____	_____
5. I used transitions to connect ideas and create unity in my writing.	_____	_____
6. I proofread and edited my composition.	_____	_____
7. I wrote a corrected copy of my work.	_____	_____

Submit the completed writing assignment and Practice exercise to your instructor for evaluation.

45.

The Short Report: A

This guide will help you to understand how a short report is written. Knowing how to write a report is essential in school and useful in many occupations. The short report is organized into three or more paragraphs. The information you use in writing the report will most likely come from one or more of the following sources:

- newspaper and magazine articles
- movies and television shows
- concerts and lectures
- biographies of famous people
- reference books containing information about places and events: past, present, or future

Practice

Read each part of the following exercise and answer all **34** questions. The model report in this guide appeared as an article in a local newspaper. The author of the report included the map on the next page to help define the subject for the reader.

MYSTERIES OF THE BERMUDA TRIANGLE

by Susan Chan

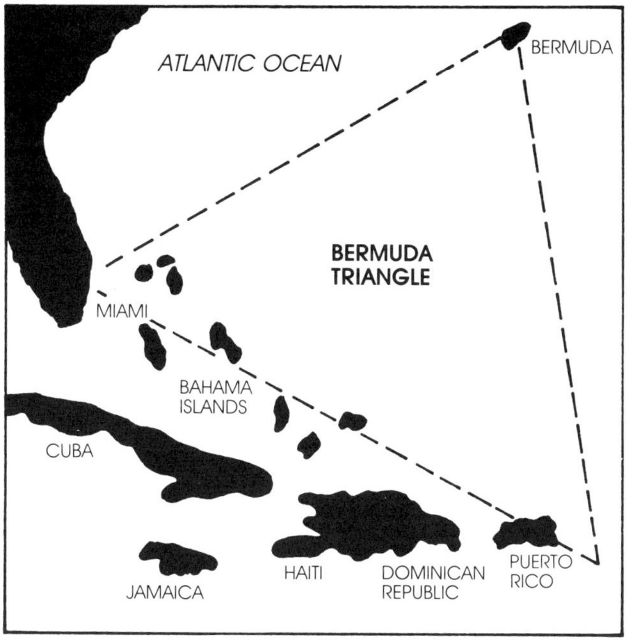

As science editor of this newspaper, it was with great interest that I attended the recent lecture presented by Charles Berlitz, author of *The Bermuda Triangle.* Mr. Berlitz talked about many of the strange and unexplained mysteries that have occurred in the Triangle. The Bermuda or Devil's Triangle is an imaginary area located off the Atlantic coast of the United States (see map). The three points of the triangle are Bermuda, southern Florida, and Puerto Rico. More than 100 planes and ships have vanished, and more than 1,000 lives have been lost in this area. Although there have been extensive searches, not one body or piece of wreckage has ever been found.

Mr. Berlitz spoke of the most well known case, the disappearance of five Navy Avenger bombers and their crews on December 5, 1945. The fourteen men were on a routine training mission off the coast of Florida. The pilots, all expert flyers, reported that every gyro and magnetic compass was "going crazy." The flight leader told the tower that they could not see land, the ocean looked strange, and that they were completely lost. An intensive search for the aircraft and crews produced no life rafts and no wreckage or oil slicks. The National Board of Inquiry said, "They vanished completely as if they had flown to Mars."

Another mystery of the sea was the disappearance of the Navy Supply Ship, U.S.S. Cyclops. The ship with a crew of 309 disappeared on March 4, 1918, in good weather. No radio messages were ever received from the ship and no wreckage was ever found. These unsolved mysteries are among hundreds that puzzle scientists and defy the laws of nature.

Many theories have been offered in an attempt to explain these unusual occurrences in the Bermuda Triangle. Some believe that there is a time-space warp leading to another dimension. Others say that electromagnetic force fields cause planes to crash and ships to be swallowed by the sea. A popular explanation is that UFOs from inner or outer space have kidnapped these vessels and their crews. Whatever the explanation, these disappearances continue to occur today. If you find this topic interesting, you will want to read Charles Berlitz's books, *The Bermuda Triangle* and *Mysteries from Forgotten Worlds*.

The science editor wrote her report based on notes she took at a lecture about the Bermuda Triangle. While she took many notes, she used only those included in the list below. Her notes are presented here without paragraphs and out of order. In the correct order, this information is an outline of the model report.

BERLITZ LECTURE NOTES

National Board of Inquiry said of bombers, "They vanished completely as if they had flown to Mars."

Over 100 planes and ships vanished thus far

Time-space warp leading to other dimensions

Pilots, expert flyers, on training mission, Florida, Dec. 5, 1945

Bermuda Triangle also known as Devil's Triangle

Navy Supply Ship U.S.S. Cyclops with crew of 309 vanished in good weather, March 4, 1918

Flight leader to tower: "Can't see land, ocean looks strange, we're completely lost."

No bodies or wreckage from any disappearances ever found

UFOs from inner or outer space kidnap vessels

Points of triangle: Bermuda, southern Florida, Puerto Rico

Electromagnetic force fields

Imaginary area off southern Atlantic coast of U.S.

Best known disappearance—five Navy Avenger bombers

More than 1,000 lives lost thus far

Search produces no life rafts, no plane wrecks, no oil slicks

Pilots report gyro and magnetic compasses "going crazy"

No radio messages, no wreckage of ship found

The first step in organizing this information is to **group** the notes by heading (topic). Do this by sorting each note into one of four groups. Refer to the model report to help you do this.

Grouping Notes

The Disappearance of Planes (six notes, order not important)

1. ______________________________
2. ______________________________
3. ______________________________
4. ______________________________
5. ______________________________
6. ______________________________

The Bermuda Triangle—What and Where (six notes, order not important)

7. ______________________________
8. ______________________________
9. ______________________________
10. ______________________________
11. ______________________________
12. ______________________________

Explanations and Theories (three notes, order not important)

13. ______________________________
14. ______________________________
15. ______________________________

The Disappearance of Ships (two notes, order not important)

16. ______________________________
17. ______________________________

After you have grouped the notes, there are two steps to **ordering** them. First, the headings are ordered as they appear in the model. This has been done for you. Second, place the notes in the order in which they appear in the model report.

Ordering Notes

I. **The Introductory Paragraph:** The Bermuda Triangle—What and Where (six notes in correct order)

18. ______________________________
19. ______________________________
20. ______________________________
21. ______________________________
22. ______________________________
23. ______________________________

II. **Development Paragraph One:** The Disappearance of Planes (six notes in correct order)

24. ______________________________
25. ______________________________
26. ______________________________
27. ______________________________
28. ______________________________
29. ______________________________

III. **Development Paragraph Two:** The Disappearance of Ships (two notes in correct order)

30. ______________________________
31. ______________________________

IV. **The Concluding Paragraph:** Explanations and Theories (three notes in correct order)

32. ______________________________
33. ______________________________
34. ______________________________

Score the Practice exercise using the Answer Key, and go on to the Composition part of this guide.

Composition

This part of the guide will help you to write a short report. Three preparatory steps in writing the short report are:

- taking notes
- grouping notes
- ordering notes

You do not have to take your own notes for this exercise. Five sets of notes are provided for you, each based on a different topic. For each topic, you are given the reason you are writing this report and the sources of your information. Choose **one** of the five topics presented in this section of the guide. Use the outlines which follow to group and order your notes, and to write your report.

Topics

The Beatles

The California Gold Rush

Amelia Earhart

Martin Luther King, Jr.

Pablo Picasso

The Beatles

Situation

You are doing a short report on the Beatles, a musical group that rose to fame in the sixties. You have located newspaper and magazine articles about the Beatles and have taken the following notes to use in writing your report.

NOTES

56,000 at Shea Stadium, summer '65, largest concert crowd

Combination of their four personalities and talents unbeatable

John Lennon, Beatles' guiding spirit, came across as most intelligent of Beatles

Known as John, Paul, George, and Ringo to fans

Four scruffy boys from Liverpool would one day set tone for an entire generation

February 1964, on Ed Sullivan show, 70 million watch

Group discovered while playing rock 'n' roll clubs in Liverpool, England

George Harrison most handsome, most dedicated musician

Beatles wrote and recorded many songs

Nobody ever matched this record of hits—mentioned in The Guiness Book of World Records

Largest television audience ever for an entertainment program

Beatles drew large crowds wherever they went on tour

Their music as popular today as when they began

In one week, top five hits on singles charts and top two albums, all by Beatles

Ringo Starr, drummer, most down to earth of Beatles

Paul McCartney, hardest worker, most romantic image

The California Gold Rush

Situation

You are writing a feature article for your school newspaper about the California Gold Rush. On a visit to Sutter's Mill, site of the first discovery, you collected books and materials for your report. You took the notes below from these sources and will use them to write a three paragraph report.

NOTES

Stood waist-deep in icy streams for days, found little gold

Presence of settlers led to growth of agriculture, commerce, transportation, and industry

People even going on crutches and stretchers

Before 1848, California sparsely populated

California now most populated state in Union

Claim jumpers: thieves who stole miners' gold and rights to their claims

California Gold Rush of 1849, America's first great migration

Thousands of people from all over the world flocked to gold fields

A few struck it rich, most miners suffered

Miners came to California, stayed to make a great state out of the land

Husbands left wives, sons left mothers, sailors left their ships

Successful miners attacked by claim jumpers

Discovery of gold at Sutter's Mill early in 1848 brought 40,000 prospectors to California

Amelia Earhart

Situation

As part of a course which is studying women in history, you have attended a documentary film at a museum. You have been asked to write a short report based on the notes you took on the film and from a biography of Amelia Earhart.

NOTES

As young girl, loved "boys" sports and games

Presented with medals by many cities: Chicago, New York, Philadelphia, Los Angeles, and Mexico City

Awarded the French Legion of Honor in Paris

August, 1932, set women's non-stop transcontinental speed record in flight from California to New Jersey

Born in Atchison, Kansas, July 24, 1898

Lost over Pacific during flight around world, July 3, 1937

Was reported that Earhart and copilot Noonan crash-landed plane in South Pacific and executed as spies by Japanese

First woman pilot to fly from Honolulu to California, 1935

Awarded Distinguished Flying Cross by United States Congress

Famous worldwide—paved the way for other female pilots

Her disappearance never adequately explained

Married George Putnam, publisher and author, who encouraged Amelia in her career

One of America's greatest heroines

Flies the Atlantic solo, in 14 hours, 56 minutes, May 21, 1932

Flights gain fame and fortune for Amelia almost overnight

Fragment of wood found with writing: "To my husband—I have crashed near Hawaii—sharks all around, A.E."

Foreign countries honor her: Mexico, France, Belgium, and England

Gold medal of the National Geographic Society presented to her by President Herbert Hoover, 1932

Martin Luther King, Jr.

Situation

You have chosen to write a short biography of a famous person as part of a course project. You took the following notes from two books about Martin Luther King, Jr.

NOTES

Organized massive civil rights March on Washington in 1963

Married Coretta Scott King in 1953, had four children

1963 designated "Man of the Year" by *Time* magazine

In Memphis, killed by assassin's bullet, April 4, 1968

World-famous leader who fought racial discrimination and prejudice

Nonviolent principles derived from Indian leader Mahatma Gandhi

Born in Atlanta, Georgia on January 15, 1929

Received Ph.D. in Theology, 1955

Plans for "Poor People's March on Washington" interrupted by trip to Memphis, Tennessee to support striking sanitation workers

Known for nonviolent philosophy in seeking social change

Baptist minister in Montgomery, Alabama, 1954-1960

Organized yearlong boycott against segregated city bus lines in Montgomery, 1955

1964, awarded Nobel Peace Prize—youngest Peace Laureate in history

Graduated from Morehouse College in 1948 with honors, 19 years old

Always supporting working man's struggle

During '63 March on Washington, King delivered his famous speech, "I Have a Dream"

Pablo Picasso

Situation

A local art magazine is sponsoring a contest for the best short biographical sketch of a famous 20th century artist. The winner will receive a $100 gift certificate for books and art supplies. You took the following notes from an encyclopedia and two books on Pablo Picasso.

NOTES

From age of seven, never without pencil in hand

Born in Malaga, Spain, October 25, 1881

His blue period depicted life of the poor

Work can be viewed in terms of both color and style

In early years, 1901 to 1908, painted first in shades of blue, and later in rose

Illustration, facing page, shows later cubist style; picture of Picasso is in foreground

Died in 1973 at age of 92

Picasso said, "To draw you must close your eyes and sing."

At age 15, admitted to well known art school by completing project in one day which took most students a month

Don Jose, his father, a painter and art teacher

Picasso painted in many styles, but cubism most important

Picasso paints famous cubist mural, "Guernica" to express his feelings about bombing of Spanish town during Civil War, 1937

He will always be considered one of the greatest artists of all time

Lived most of his adult life in France

During rose period, painted many circus people who were his friends and models

"The Old Guitarist" painted during blue period, on display in Art Institute of Chicago

First phase of cubism, 1907 to 1912, shows all dimensions of an object: width, height, and depth

Later phase of cubism, after 1912, shows objects and people in two dimensions, flat, without depth

First, study the notes for your topic and group them into categories (headings) that you create.

Grouping Notes

Heading: ______________________________

(Number of notes: ______, order not important)

____

____

____

____

____

Heading: ______________________________

(Number of notes: ______, order not important)

____

____

____

____

____

Heading: ______________________________

(Number of notes: ______, order not important)

____

____

____

____

____

Heading: ______________________________

(Number of notes: ______, order not important)

____

____

____

____

____

Now, organize the notes you have grouped. First, **determine the order of the headings:** introduction, development, and conclusion. This report may have one or more development paragraphs. Next, **order your notes** so that there is meaning and continuity to each sequence.

Ordering Notes

I. Introductory Paragraph: ______________________
(list notes in order) (heading)

____
____
____
____
____

II. Development Paragraph: ______________________
(list notes in order) (heading)

____
____
____
____
____

III. Development Paragraph: ______________________
(list notes in order) (heading)

____
____
____
____
____

IV. Concluding Paragraph: ______________________
(list notes in order) (heading)

____
____
____
____
____

After you have grouped and ordered your notes, follow the Short Report Outline to present the information you have organized.

Short Report Outline

I. The Introductory Paragraph

A. Your opening sentences let the reader know your topic, the audience you are addressing, and your position as the author. This information may be presented in any order.

Example In the model report on the Bermuda Triangle the author:

1. states the topic (the Bermuda Triangle).
2. speaks to her audience (the readers of the article).
3. tells the reader her status as writer (science editor of the newspaper).

B. Define the topic: who, what, where, when.

C. Write a conclusion that leads the reader from the introduction to the development portion of the essay (transition).

II. The Development Paragraph(s)—For each paragraph:

A. State the topic of **this** paragraph.

B. Offer specifics: facts, details, and information pertaining to the topic of **this** paragraph.

C. Briefly summarize the major point of **this** paragraph.

III. The Concluding Paragraph

A. Bring the reader up to date by referring to the current status of the topic of your report.

B. Express your personal view with regard to the topic.

C. Write a conclusion for your report.

Use the Checklist to help you review and revise your writing. Do this for all drafts and your final copy.

Checklist	**Yes**	**No**
1. I chose one of five topics provided and grouped the notes into categories (headings) that I created.	____	____
2. I organized my headings and notes in a sequence that has meaning and continuity.	____	____
3. I followed the Short Report Outline to present information.	____	____
4. I used transitions to connect ideas and create unity in my writing.	____	____
5. I proofread and edited my report.	____	____
6. I wrote a corrected copy of my work.	____	____

Submit the completed writing assignment and Practice exercise to your instructor for evaluation.

46.

The Short Report: B

The first part of this guide gives you an opportunity to practice your grammar, usage, and punctuation. It can also be used to improve your spelling, learn new words, and sharpen your reading comprehension skills. These activities will help to improve your writing.

Skills Practice

Choose one or more of the following exercises and answer at least **thirty** questions:

A **corrective** exercise recommended by your instructor.

A **spelling** exercise from available materials.

A **vocabulary** exercise from available materials.

A **reading comprehension** exercise from available materials.

Record the number of questions you complete, and score the exercise using available answer keys. Then go on to the Composition part of this guide.

Composition

This section of the guide provides additional practice in writing a short report. Write a report on the topic of your choice. Your instructor may also suggest topics. Information for your report may come from one or more sources as listed in the very beginning of The Short Report guide.

The three preparatory steps in writing the short report are taking notes, grouping notes, and ordering notes.

Taking Notes

Your notes should define the topic with specific information: who, what, where, when, how, why.

Write your notes on **index cards** according to the steps outlined here. Notes taken initially on notepaper can later be transferred to index cards.

1. Write one note per card.
2. Indicate the source in the upper right hand corner.
3. Write the subject in the center of the card. Your note is written just below this title.
4. If your source is a book, write the page number on which the information appears. Record this in the lower left corner of the card.
5. Write on only one side of the card.

SAMPLE NOTE CARD

> The Bermuda Triangle
> by Charles Berlitz
>
> Disappearance of Ships
>
> December 1967: Revonoc, all-weather forty-six foot racing yacht; disappeared within sight of land near the Florida Keys.
>
> Page 56

Grouping Notes

In order to group your notes, you need to establish headings. Write each heading on a separate index card and spread these out on a table. Place each note card under the most appropriate heading. Do this until you are satisfied with the way your notes are grouped. Use this procedure for grouping information whenever you take notes for a report.

Ordering Notes

First, arrange the headings in order as they will appear in the report: introduction, development, and conclusion. Next, order the note cards for each heading to give meaning and continuity to each sequence.

When you have completed the three preparatory steps above, you are ready to write your report. Follow the Short Report Outline to present the information you have organized.

Short Report Outline

I. The Introductory Paragraph

   A. Your opening sentences let the reader know your topic, the audience you are addressing, and your status as the author. This information may be presented in any order.

   B. Define the topic: who, what, where, when.

   C. Write a conclusion that leads the reader from the introduction to the development portion of the essay (transition).

II. The Development Paragraph(s)—For each paragraph:

A. State the topic of **this** paragraph.

B. Offer specifics: facts, details, and information pertaining to the topic of **this** paragraph.

C. Briefly summarize the major point of **this** paragraph.

III. The Concluding Paragraph

A. Bring the reader up to date by referring to the current status of the topic of your report.

B. Express your personal view with regard to the topic.

C. Write a conclusion for your report.

Use the Checklist to help you review and revise your writing. Do this for all drafts and your final copy.

Checklist	**Yes**	**No**
1. I selected a topic and used one or more sources.	_____	_____
2. I completed the three preparatory steps for writing a report: taking notes, grouping notes, and ordering notes.	_____	_____
3. I followed the Short Report Outline to write my report.	_____	_____
4. I used transitions to connect ideas and create unity in my writing.	_____	_____
5. I proofread and edited my report	_____	_____
6. I wrote a corrected copy of my work.	_____	_____

Submit the completed writing assignment and Practice exercise to your instructor for evaluation.

47.

The Research Paper

This guide will help you to understand how to write a research paper. The skills you have acquired in writing the short report are also used in the research paper. While the form of both is the same—introduction, development, conclusion—the research report has more development paragraphs. Knowing how to write a research paper is essential in school and useful in many occupations.

Practice

Read each part of the following exercise and answer all **79** questions. The model research paper explains Transactional Analysis, an interesting theory about human behavior. Note that the model begins with a cover sheet which serves as a title page for the paper.

Transactional Analysis

by

Marcia Thomas

Psychology 101

Mr. David Morse

December 6, 1998

Transactional Analysis (TA) is an exciting and practical way of learning about yourself and how you interact with others. Transactions can take the form of words, gestures, or physical contact. When people communicate with one another, they are involved in a transaction. Analysis explains the transaction and helps us to understand why people are speaking, gesturing, or making physical contact. TA can be used at work, in school, in your personal life, and wherever people interact. This paper will introduce you to some of the main ideas of TA theory and show how they can be useful to you.

Imagine that there are three people inside of you. Each of these people is you, at different times. These three people think for you, feel for you, and act for you. They are not actually people, but three different ways in which you see the world. Dr. Eric Berne called these "Ego (Self) States" and named them the Parent, Adult, and Child (Steere 6-7). The Parent in each of us tells us what we're supposed to do, for better or for worse. The Adult is the thinking part of a person, regardless of age. The Child is the feeling self. For any decision that has to be made, the Parent has beliefs about it, the Adult has thoughts about it, and the Child has feelings about it. All three ego states play a part in our view of the world.

The Parent ego state is made up of behavior and attitudes copied from parents and other authority figures. Their messages are carried in our heads "on tape." The Parent can be either critical or nurturing. The Critical Parent is authoritarian,

judgmental, and moralistic. The Nurturing Parent is caring, supportive, and understanding. The Nurturing Parent acts out of concern for others, while the Critical Parent acts out of a need to control (Woollams and Brown 27). When you help a friend, you're in your Nurturing Parent. If you scold him for asking for help, you're in your Critical Parent.

The Adult ego state is often called the "computer." It collects and stores information and figures out answers to problems. The Adult thinks clearly and makes logical decisions. Of the three ego states, the Adult is the best evaluator of reality because it is not clouded by emotion. The Adult is interested, observant, and evaluative. The Adult can evaluate the emotions and demands of both the Child and Parent ego states. The more you use your Adult, the better it functions. Right now, by reading this page, you are using your Adult to learn.

The Child ego state is the part of us that feels. A person, regardless of age, acting from his Child ego state might be inquisitive, affectionate, selfish, cruel, playful, or manipulative (James and Jongeward 127). The Child ego state is made up of three parts: the Natural Child, the Little Professor, and the Adapted Child. The Natural Child is really the infant still inside each of us. It is like a self-centered baby who is affectionate when its needs are met and angry when they are not met. The Little Professor, the creative and intuitive part of your Child ego state, builds sandcastles and intuits the meaning of a friend's nod. The

Adapted Child seeks the approval of others, especially parent or authority figures. Doing what others ask may lead us to learn about sharing, taking turns, and being sociable. On the other hand, always doing what others ask inevitably leads us to suppress our feelings. The Natural Child, the Little Professor, and the Adapted Child are three different ways that people express their feelings.

If you know which ego state you are in during a transaction—Parent, Adult, or Child—then understanding and getting along with others becomes easier. There are basically four different ways of identifying ego states (Freed and Freed 38). One way is to know how you feel. If you are feeling happy, sad, or angry, your Child is in charge. If you stop feeling because you hear yourself saying, "Don't be unhappy," your Parent is in charge. When you start thinking about why you feel a particular way, the Adult is taking over.

Another way to figure out which ego state you are in is by listening to the words you use. You are in your Parent when you use words like: "Don't. You should. You must. I'll take care of you. You're okay. Have a nice day." You are in your Adult when you use words like: "What? Why? How? I think. Let me check it out." You are in your Child when you use words like: "I want. I don't care. No! I won't. Wow! Yummy! Darn (or worse)."

A third way to know what state you are in is to look at how you are acting. If you are screaming, crying, or daydreaming, you

are in your Child. If you are scolding, helping a friend, or giving an order, you're in your Parent. If you are reading, answering questions, or trying to figure out which ego state is in charge, you're in your Adult.

The fourth way is to be aware of how others are acting toward you. If people are often critical of you, you are probably in your Child with them. Switch to your Adult and see what happens. If you find yourself being critical of others, you probably want and need something. Take the pressure off by doing something pleasurable for yourself. When you do, you'll find yourself in your Natural Child. When you're not feeling good or getting what you want in a situation, switch ego states. Often, making a change leads to more enjoyable and meaningful transactions.

Every transaction involves an exchange of strokes. A stroke is any act by someone else that lets you know they are there. It may be a look, a word, or a touch. Strokes can be positive or negative. Positive strokes include compliments, smiles, encouragement, and touching that feels good (hugs). Negative strokes include put-downs, criticism, teasing, and touching that feels bad (slaps). We all need strokes to survive. Infants who do not experience enough touch suffer mentally and physically, and may even die as a result of stroke deprivation (Spitz 53). Although we prefer positive strokes, people will take negative strokes over nothing at all.

People's hunger for strokes often leads them to get strokes any way they can. Some straightforward ways of getting strokes are by working, having fun, and being close to others. Crooked ways of getting strokes involve playing psychological games. Games are ways of getting strokes when we don't think we can get them any other way. We've got to con or trick people into giving us strokes. "See what you made me do" is the first line of a game in which you blame others for your mistakes. In this way you collect anger strokes for being one up on others. "Poor Me" is a game in which you complain to others about your situation. In this way you collect sympathy strokes for being one down to others. "If you find yourself going through a similar set of behaviors with the same or different people, and things always wind up badly for you, maybe you're playing a game. Most of us do until we learn how to quit and come on straight" (Freed 51).

Now that you have been introduced to Transactional Analysis, try applying what you have learned. When you are feeling bad or not getting what you want from transactions with others, change the outcome by switching to another ego state. You'll notice that the strokes you get from honest transactions feel much better than those you get by playing games. When we give up the need to be one up or one down to others, we can all be winners.

BIBLIOGRAPHY

Freed, Alvyn. *T. A. for Teens*. Sacramento: Jalmar Press, 1976.

Freed, Alvyn and Margaret Freed. *T. A. for Kids*. Sacramento: Jalmar Press, 1977.

James, Muriel and Dorothy Jongeward. *Born to Win*. Philippines: Addison-Wesley Publishing Company, 1971.

Spitz, Renee. "Hospitalism: Genesis of Psychiatric Conditions in Early Childhood," *Psychoanalytic Study of the Child*. 1 (1945) : 53-74.

Steere, David. *Bodily Expressions in Psychology*. New York: Brunner/Mazel, 1982.

Woollams, Stan and Michael Brown. *The Total Handbook of Transactional Analysis*. Englewood Cliffs: Prentice-Hall, 1979.

The model paper you have just read has twelve paragraphs. The list below contains the twelve paragraph headings out of their proper sequence. Arrange these headings in the same order as the paragraphs appear in the model. Use the outline on the next page to help you do this.

Paragraph Headings

Exchange of Strokes: Positive and Negative

Applying What You Have Learned

Transactional Analysis Defined

Three People Inside of You: Parent, Adult, Child

Know Your Ego State: Your Feelings

Hunger for Strokes: Games

Parent Ego State Defined

Know Your Ego State: Your Actions

Know Your Ego State: Other's Reactions to You

Adult Ego State Defined

Know Your Ego State: Your Words

Child Ego State Defined

The **introduction** to the model report is completed in one paragraph. Place the heading for the first paragraph next to the words *The Introduction* in the outline.

The **development** portion of the paper contains ten paragraphs (A-J). Place the heading for each paragraph in correct sequence.

The **conclusion** of the report is presented in one paragraph. Place the heading for the last paragraph next to the words *The Conclusion* in the outline.

Outline for Ordering Paragraph Headings

1. I. The Introduction ______________________________

II. The Development

2. A. ______________________________
3. B. ______________________________
4. C. ______________________________
5. D. ______________________________
6. E. ______________________________
7. F. ______________________________
8. G. ______________________________
9. H. ______________________________
10. I. ______________________________
11. J. ______________________________

12. III. The Conclusion ______________________________

In the exercise that follows, the paragraph headings of the model research paper are presented in order. The notes for each paragraph are out of sequence. Order the notes as they appear in the report.

Order the notes within each set as they appear in each paragraph. Write the number **1** next to the first note in a paragraph, the number **2** next to the second note, and so on. The first set has been placed in the correct order for you. Do the same for the remaining sets of notes.

Transactional Analysis Defined

13. __**3**__ analysis: explains the transaction

14. __**4**__ TA useful wherever people interact

15. __**1**__ exciting and practical way to learn about yourself, others

16. __**2**__ transactions: words, gestures, physical contact

Three People Inside You: Parent, Adult, Child

17. ______ Child—the feeling self

18. ______ Parent—tells us what to do

19. ______ Dr. Eric Berne's Ego States: Parent, Adult, Child

20. ______ Adult—thinking part of person

21. ______ three *people* think, feel, and act for you

22. ______ ego states shape our view of world

Parent Ego State Defined

23. ______ Critical Parent: authoritarian, judgmental, moralistic

24. ______ messages in our heads *on tape*

25. ______ concern for vs. control of others

26. ______ Parent ego state copies authority figures

27. ______ Nurturing Parent: caring, supportive, understanding

Adult Ego State Defined

28. ______ Adult thinks clearly, makes logical decisions
29. ______ Adult ego state best evaluator of reality
30. ______ the more you use Adult, the better it functions
31. ______ Adult evaluates both Child and Parent ego states
32. ______ Adult ego state like a computer

Child Ego State Defined

33. ______ Child: Natural Child, Little Professor, Adapted Child
34. ______ doing what others ask—sharing and being social
35. ______ Adapted Child—seeks approval of others
36. ______ three different ways people express feelings
37. ______ Child ego state *feels*
38. ______ Child ego state, regardless of age, can be inquisitive, affectionate, selfish, cruel, playful, manipulative
39. ______ Natural Child—infant still within us
40. ______ always doing what others ask—suppressing feelings
41. ______ Little Professor—creative and intuitive

Know Your Ego State: Your Feelings

42. ______ happy, sad, angry—Child in charge
43. ______ *Don't*—Parent in charge
44. ______ knowing which ego state you're in—Parent, Adult, Child
45. ______ know how you feel
46. ______ why you feel that way—Adult taking over
47. ______ four different ways to identify ego states

Know Your Ego State: Your Words

48. ______ Adult words: *What, Why, How, I think*

49. ______ listen to your words

50. ______ Child words: *I want, I don't care, Wow!, Darn!*

51. ______ Parent words: *Don't, You should, I'll take care of you*

Know Your Ego State: Your Actions

52. ______ figuring out which ego state is in charge—Adult

53. ______ reading, asking or answering questions—Adult

54. ______ look at how you are acting

55. ______ screaming, crying, daydreaming—Child

56. ______ scolding, helping, ordering—Parent

Know Your Ego State: Others' Reactions

57. ______ get into your Natural Child

58. ______ switching ego states leads to more meaningful transactions

59. ______ if people critical of you, you're probably in Child

60. ______ be aware of others' actions toward you

61. ______ if you're critical of others, you probably need something

Exchange of Strokes: Positive and Negative

62. ______ strokes are necessary for survival
63. ______ negative strokes: criticism, teasing, slaps
64. ______ negative strokes better than no strokes at all
65. ______ transaction involves exchange of strokes
66. ______ strokes are recognition: a look, a word, a touch
67. ______ positive strokes: compliments, smiles, hugs
68. ______ strokes can be positive or negative
69. ______ positive strokes are preferred
70. ______ infants deprived of touch suffer mentally, physically, and may even die

Hunger for Strokes: Games

71. ______ getting crooked strokes—playing psychological games
72. ______ *Poor me*—complaining to collect sympathy strokes
73. ______ getting straightforward strokes: working, having fun, being close to others
74. ______ "If you find yourself going through a similar set of behaviors with the same or different people, and things always wind up badly for you, maybe you're playing a game. Most of us do until we learn how to quit and come on straight."
75. ______ people hunger for strokes

Applying What You Have Learned

76. ______ strokes from honest transactions feel better
77. ______ feeling bad, switch to another ego state
78. ______ we can all be winners
79. ______ try applying what you've learned

Score the Practice exercise using the Answer Key, and go on to the Composition part of this guide.

Composition

This part of the guide will help you to write a research paper. In order to write a good paper, it is important to be organized. The following notes spell out, in detail, the steps to take in writing a research report.

Selecting a Topic

There are many ways to choose a topic. You may already have one in mind. Your instructor may offer suggestions. You can also use *The Subject Guide to Books in Print* or other reference sources.

One way of choosing a topic is to make a list of the subjects that interest you. Next to each, write those ideas that occur to you in relation to the subject. See the example below. Your ideas will lead you to a topic for your research report.

Subject (general)	**Ideas** (specific)
Antiques	weapons, toys, cars, clothes
Energy	solar, nuclear, geothermal, psychic
Geography	Hawaii, Puerto Rico, Himalayas, Amazon River
Famous performers	Michael Jackson, Marilyn Monroe, Clint Eastwood, Diana Ross
Inventions	the lightbulb, the wheel, the telephone, the computer

Organizing Your Information

Once you have decided on a topic, use the library's resources for gathering information and taking notes.

1. take notes on index cards
2. determine paragraph headings
3. group notes by heading
4. order headings as they will appear in report
5. order notes under each heading

Writing the Paper

When you have selected a topic, taken notes, grouped your notes and ordered them, you are ready to write your report. Follow. the Research Paper Outline to present the information you have organized.

Research Paper Outline

I. The Introductory Paragraph

  A. Begin with a strong statement or question that appeals to the reader's interest.

  B. Define the topic for your audience: who, what, where, when, how.

  C. State a plan of development for the report and provide a transition to the next paragraph.

II. The Development Paragraphs: For each paragraph:

  A. State the topic of **this** paragraph.

  B. Offer specifics: facts, details, explanations, and information pertaining to the topic of **this** paragraph.

  C. Briefly summarize the major point of **this** paragraph.

III. The Concluding Paragraph

A. Bring the reader up to date by referring to the current status of the topic of your report.

B. Express your personal view with regard to the topic.

C. Write a conclusion for your report.

IV. Documentation

A. In the body of your paper, each reference that appears in parentheses follows the same author reference system. This parenthetical reference includes the author's last name and the page number on which the author's specific words appear, e.g. (Spitz 53).

B. The bibliography page lists the books, journals, and magazines you used in doing the research paper. This list is alphabetized by author's last name. Each citation also includes the publication title, the location (city) and name of the publisher, and the copyright year. Citations for journal articles include the name of the journal in which the article appears. See the entry for Spitz in the Bibliography.

C. A complete guide to writing the research paper may be found in the following reference work:

Gibaldi, Joseph and Walter S. Achtert. *MLA Handbook for Writers of Research Papers.* New York: The Modern Language Association of America, 1988.

Note: In print, the title of a work cited will be italicized. In a typed manuscript, the title will be underlined if no italics are available.

Use the Checklist to help you review and revise your writing. Do this for all drafts and your final copy. Type your research paper on unlined bond paper. Double-space and use only one side of the page.

Checklist	**Yes**	**No**
1. I selected a topic, took notes, grouped my notes and ordered them.	____	____
2. I followed the Research Paper Outline to write my report.	____	____
3. I used the correct form for citing references in the body of my paper.	____	____
4. I documented my sources in a Bibliography.	____	____
5. I used transitions to connect ideas and create unity in my writing.	____	____
6. I proofread and edited my research paper.	____	____
7. I typed a corrected copy of my work.	____	____

Submit the completed writing assignment and Practice exercise to your instructor for evaluation.

48.

Writing Appraisal II

The first part of this guide gives you an opportunity to practice your grammar, usage, and punctuation. It can also be used to improve your spelling, learn new words, and sharpen your reading comprehension skills. These activities will help to improve your writing.

Skills Practice

Choose one or more of the following exercises and answer at least **thirty** questions:

A **corrective** exercise recommended by your instructor.

A **spelling** exercise from available materials.

A **vocabulary** exercise from available materials.

A **reading comprehension** exercise from available materials.

Record the number of questions you complete, and score the exercise using available answer keys. Then go on to the Composition part of this guide.

Composition

This exercise will provide you and your instructor with a sample of your writing at the end of this program. Your instructor's evaluation will allow you to measure your progress over the course of the program. Write **three** paragraphs according to the instructions given.

Narration Write a paragraph of **five** complete sentences that tells a story about one of the following events:

an embarrassing situation
something that changed my life
the best day of my life
a frightening experience

Description Write a paragraph of **five** complete sentences that describes one of the following subjects:

a face
a bakery
a cut finger
a sunset

Explanation Write a paragraph of **five** complete sentences that explains how to do one of the following:

apply make-up
catch a fish
cook something
help someone who is choking

Submit the completed writing assignment and Skills Practice exercise to your instructor for evaluation.

Answer Key

Contents

Using the Dictionary

1. surprise
2. an attack made without warning
3. something that surprises
4. the state of being surprised
5. One of two or more words that have the same meaning. (Variations of this definition are acceptable.)
6. astonishment
7. unusual
8. nightclub
9. fly
10. peaceful
11. confusion
12. confront
13. digest
14. entrance
15. hollow
16. kitten
17. middle
18. owl
19. quiet
20. sugar
21. write
22. pioneer
23. pleasant
24. plenty
25. predict
26. prepare
27. pretty
28. probe
29. pronounce
30. proud
31. pure
32. a
33. s
34. b
35. b
36. s
37. s
38. a
39. b
40. a
41. s
42. b
43. a

The Complete Sentence

1. If your answer is a complete sentence, you are correct. Some sample answers are:

   a. The boy is washing the car.
   b. I saw the boy washing the car.
   c. The boy washing the car is in my class.
   d. Is the boy washing the car?

2. If your answer is a complete sentence, you are correct. Some sample answers are:

   a. The truck is going too fast.
   b. She saw the truck going too fast.
   c. The truck going too fast is going to crash!
   d. Isn't the truck going too fast?

3. This morning I got a flat tire.

4. How did you get the flat tire?

5. Oh no! My car has another flat!

6. My car has a flat tire, and I may have to walk to work.

7. I would have changed the tire, but I didn't know how to do it.

8. Can you change the tire, or do you want to call the service station?

9. She waited by the side of the road; many cars passed by without stopping.

10. He saw a white cloth tied to the radio antenna; he knew she needed help.

11. The man was kind; he changed the tire.

12. the little girl

13. she pulled the cat's tail

14. the bike

15. it races down the hill

16. the ball

17. on the table

18. the boy

19. at the movies

20. I can come to the party, (and) I'll bring a cake.

21. I can help you with your work later, (but) I want to rest now.

22. Do you want to eat at eleven, (or) would you rather eat at twelve?

23. If my little sister stays home, I am going to the beach.

24. When I swim, I like to wear goggles.

25. While we're on vacation, my brother and I plan to go sailing.

26. I am going to the beach if my little sister stays home.

27. I like to wear goggles when I swim.

28. My brother and I plan to go sailing while we're on vacation.

Answering Questions

1. no
2. no
3. yes
4. yes
5. no
6. yes
7. yes
8. yes
9. yes
10. no
11. no
12. yes
13. yes
14. no
15. no
16. no
17. no
18. yes

Transitional Words and Phrases

There are one or more correct answers for each blank.

1. Afterwards
   Eventually
   First
   Later
   Next
2. after
   before
   once

3. after
afterwards
eventually
in the meantime
later
meanwhile
next
soon
then

4. After
Afterwards
Eventually
Later
Now
Soon
Then

5. First
Now

6. After
Afterwards
Next
Second
Then

7. Afterwards
Meanwhile
Next
Now
Then

8. After
Afterwards
Later
Next
Now
Then

9. if
since
because

10. Because
Since
While

11. because
if
since

12. Even though
While

13. also
nevertheless

14. and

15. because
if
since

16. As long as
Since
Due to the fact that
In view of the fact that

17. As a result of
Because of
Due to
In view of

18. Consequently
For these reasons
Hence
In conclusion
So
Summarily
Thus

19. as a result of
because of
due to

20. As a result
Evidently
For this reason

21. Consequently
Evidently
In conclusion
It is evident
Thus

22. although
but
though
yet

23. Although
Though
While

24. but
however
yet

25. Unless

26. but

27. Conversely
However
In contrast
On the contrary
On the other hand
Yet

28. unless

Sentence Combining

1. Sunday
2. afternoon
3. autumn
4. early
5. perfect
6. stroll
7. park
8. leaves
9. trees
10. covering
11. colors
12. couple
13. young
14. holding hands
15. sparkling
16. rays
17. sun
18. brilliant
19. painting
20. alive
21. people
22. colors

Paragraph Development

1. Anyone can build a campfire.
2. You begin with some wood shavings or small, dry twigs.
3. On top of that you place some larger twigs or thin branches.
4. When you begin to pile on the heavier wooden pieces, use a crisscross pattern.
5. This leaves plenty of space for the fire to come through.
6. Light the wood shavings or dried twigs with a match, and the job is done.
7. There is nothing complicated about building a campfire.
8. When I was little, my older sister was always trying to scare me.
9. She would jump out, screaming, from under the staircase.
10. She would turn the lights off and hold a flashlight under her chin.
11. She told frightening tales (stories).
12. Now, I laugh whenever I recall how easily my sister could scare me when I was young.

13. When I looked through our family photo album last Sunday, I was reminded of all the good times we had during our summer vacations.

14–16. Any three of the following are correct: fishing, taking pictures (photography), water skiing, boating, visiting amusement parks, riding the water flume

17. Summer vacations are great because I always have a wonderful time.

The Narrative Paragraph

1. disobedient; ill-tempered
2. It is late afternoon.
3. "It was getting dark fast by then"
4. The story takes place in the woods.
5. "didn't seem to be anything alive around; stumbled over a hidden rock; scratched and sore all over"
6. The author is writing about a young person.
7. "He almost cried; he began to shoot the gun just to get used to it."
8. He's trying to get used to shooting a gun.
9. "he began to shoot the gun just to get used to it"
10. The character feels like crying. He is unhappy and scared.
11. "almost cried; not very happy; He was scared, too, and he said a prayer a minute"
12. The character in this paragraph consoles himself by praying.
13. "he said a prayer a minute and meant every word of what he said."

The Descriptive Paragraph

1. towered thirty feet above half the trees; great evil god

2. none 3. none 4. none 5. none

6. leg, piston, thousand pounds of white bone, thick ropes of muscle.

7. none 8. none 9. a piston moving

10. thick ropes 11. thigh, ton of meat 12. none

13. none 14. none 15. none

16. two delicate arms dangled; hands pick up men like toys

17. none 18. none 19. none

20. hands that pick up men 21. snake neck coiled

22. none 23. none 24. none 25. none

26. mouth hung open; teeth like daggers

27. none

28. none

29. none

30. teeth like daggers

31. eyes rolled

32. none

33. none

34. none

35. none

36. They (the eyes) showed hunger

37. hunger

38. none

39. none

40. none

41. closed mouth; death grin

42. none

43. none

44. closed its mouth

45. none

The Expository Paragraph

1. E	2. I	3. A	4. D	5. F
6. B	7. G	8. H	9. C	

10. The subject of this paragraph is how to prepare for spearfishing.

11. The author presents information in a sequence of preparatory steps.

12. fifteen

13. eleven

For questions 14–23, the following words in any order are correct:

14–23.	although	so/so that	before	then
	and	if	when	
	first of all	next	once	

Using Examples

1. Few Americans will walk anywhere if they can help it, either for practical purpose or for pleasure.

Questions 2–7 can be in any order.

2. banking
3. mailing letters
4. watching films
5. store shopping
6. restaurant service
7. "drive-in" church

8. cars: Corvette, Ford, Mercedes, Toyota
9. entertainment: concert, disco, movie, museum
10. feelings: angry, delighted, excited, scared
11. food: cheeseburger, pizza, salad, tacos
12. planets: Earth, Mars, Pluto, Saturn

13. relatives: aunt, brother, cousin, grandmother

14. seasons: fall, spring, summer, winter

15. sports: basketball, golf, soccer, tennis

16. other: lipstick, purple, sailboat, twelve

Using Definition

1. D 2. E 3. B 4. C 5. F

6. G 7. A 8. the guitar

9. a handheld, stringed, musical instrument made of wood

10. played by pressing strings against frets with one hand while strumming guitar with other

11. none 12. musical instrument

13. made of wood; strings of nylon or steel

14. body, sound hole, finger board, frets, strings, bridge, and tuning pegs

15. box, flat, hollow, pear or figure eight, circular opening

16. handheld; long piece of wood 17. none

18. hollow inside 19. banjo, mandolin, ukulele, violin

Comparison and Contrast

1. apples and oranges 2. fruits 3. seven

4. any five of the following: similar, both, however, while, but, differ, whereas, most important

	APPLES	ORANGES
5.	not applicable	not applicable
6.	round	round
7.	red, green, or yellow	orange
8.	cold	hot
9.	juicy and delicious	juicy and delicious
10.	small	small
11.	thin	thick
12.	not applicable	not applicable
13.	edible	inedible
14.	nutritious	nutritious
15.	not applicable	not applicable

16. comparison
17. contrast
18. both
19. comparison
20. contrast
21. contrast
22. both
23. contrast
24. comparison
25. comparison
26. both
27. both
28. comparison

Cause and Effect

1. five
2. as a result, because, when, so that, if
3. effect, cause
4. cause, effect
5. cause, effect
6. effect, cause
7. cause, effect
8. cause, effect
9. effect, cause
10. effect, cause
11. cause, effect
12. effect, cause
13. effect, cause

The Persuasive Paragraph

1. I puffed in the face of danger, even though I was aware that smoking is linked to lung cancer, heart disease, and other potentially fatal diseases.

2. six

3. He didn't enjoy eating.
   His social contacts didn't like smoke in their faces.
   Smoking cut his energy level.
   He had trouble exercising.
   He had trouble playing sports.
   He had trouble walking up stairs.

4. If you smoke cigarettes and want to stop, you can.

5. Is this beginning to sound familiar?

6. You can do the same for yourself!

7. I finally quit smoking so that I could enjoy the rest of my life.

8. You can do the same for yourself!

9. fact
10. opinion
11. fact
12. opinion
13. opinion
14. fact
15. opinion
16. opinion
17. fact
18. fact
19. opinion
20. fact
21. opinion
22. fact
23. opinion

The Three Paragraph Essay

1. Have you ever tried to wish away a cold?

2. The common cold, with its accompanying cough, fever, aches and pains, can be effectively treated by you.

3. If you follow the advice presented here, you can minimize the discomforts of a cold.

4. There are three basic steps to follow in curing the common cold.
5. six
6. Sleep, moist air to breathe, and liquids to drink will help to make you well again.
7. Take time to care for yourself when you have a cold.
8. You will be rewarded by feeling healthier, sooner.
9. You may not be able to wish away a cold, but you can make yourself feel a lot better.

The Short Story

1. "The Boy Who Painted Christ Black"
2. John Henrik Clarke
3. c
4. a
5. b
6. d
7. e
8. b
9. a
10. c
11. b
12. a
13. b
14. c
15. a

Characterization

1. A
2. B
3. D
4. A
5. A
6. C
7. D
8. C
9. B
10. B
11. D
12. D
13. D
14. A
15. A
16. B
17. D
18. B
19. C
20. B
21. A
22. D
23. D
24. C
25. A
26. B
27. D

Writing Dialogue

1. "Look at the creature coming out of the peach," said the girl.
2. The father said, "That's where Gaston lives."
3. "He's ugly!" exclaimed the girl.
4. "He's quite handsome for his kind," replied the father.
5. "Where will Gaston live now?" asked the girl.
6. "Gaston is out in the world," answered the father, "and on his own now."
7. "I want a peach," said the girl, "only if somebody is in the seed."
8. "I think you like Gaston," said the father. "I'll try to get you another peach just like that one."
9. The girl's mother said, "Let me speak to your father."
10. "He's not here," said the girl. "He's gone to get me a peach."
11. "Is he getting you just one peach?" asked the mother.
12. The girl answered, "He's going to find me a peach with people in it."
13. The mother asked the girl, "Is your father funny?"
14. "He doesn't holler when he sees a bug crawling out of a peach," said the girl.
15. "Where is Gaston?" asked the father when he returned.
16. "I squashed him," the girl replied.
17. "Why did you do that?" he asked.
18. "I don't want a peach anymore," said the girl sadly.
19. "I feel a little bit like Gaston," said the father.

Conflict and Plot

1. B
2. A
3. A
4. E
5. D
6. C
7. C
8. B
9. A/B
10. A
11. E
12. C
13. C
14. A
15. A
16. E
17. A
18. C
19. G
20. E
21. H
22. F
23. I
24. A
25. B
26. J
27. C
28. K
29. D
30. G—exposition
31. E—exposition
32. H—exposition
33. F—conflict
34. I—conflict
35. A—complication
36. B—complication
37. J—complication
38. C—climax
39. K—resolution
40. D—conclusion

Understanding Theme

1. characterization, b
2. conflict, a
3. setting, b
4. characterization, b
5. conflict, b
6. characterization, c
7. setting, c
8. characterization, c
9. characterization, d
10. conflict, d
11. setting, f
12. conflict, f
13. conflict, e
14. characterization, e or f
15. characterization, f
16. conflict, g
17. characterization, h
18. conflict, g
19. characterization, g
20. setting, h
21. conflict, g

Point of View

1. a
2. b
3. c
4. c
5. b
6. c
7. b
8. b
9. a
10. c
11. c
12. c
13. b
14. a
15. b
16. c
17. b
18. a
19. c
20. a
21. c
22. a
23. b
24. c
25. a
26. c
27. b
28. a
29. a
30. b
31. c
32. b
33. c
34. b
35. c
36. a
37. b

Business Letter: Employment

1. a
2. b
3. b
4. a
5. d
6. b
7. C
8. A
9. B
10. A
11. C
12. B
13. A
14. C
15. B
16. why you are writing
17. the position applied for
18. how you heard of the opening
19. qualifications to do this work
20. reasons for wanting this job
21. relevant career goals
22. reference to enclosed resume

23. request for an interview
24. how you can be reached

Business Letter: Ordering

1. street address
2. state
3. capital letters
4. comma
5. zip code
6. date
7. year
8. day
9. inside address
10. name
11. cities
12. state
13. greeting
14. Dear Sir or Madam
15. : colon
16. body
17. explains
18. two
19. product
20. cost
21. sent
22. closing
23. comma
24. lower case letter
25. sign
26. signature
27. B
28. A
29. A
30. A
31. B
32. B
33. indicate the product you are ordering
34. brief description of product, including model or reference number
35. special instructions, if any
36. how you plan to pay for merchandise
37. reference to postage and handling
38. how you would like product shipped

Business Letter: Complaint

1. A
2. B
3. B
4. B
5. A
6. A
7. date you ordered product
8. description of product and model number
9. cost of product, including shipping

10. date you received product
11. description of product received
12. what you want seller to do

The Persuasive Essay

1. As an employee of this company, I would like to suggest that the Personnel Department offer a program in stress management.
2. Maria Arias, Director of Personnel
3. a stress management program for employees
4. Jim Kennedy, Sales Manager
5. improved productivity; reduced absenteeism
6. I believe such a program would benefit our company and its employees.
7. If our company were to implement a stress management program, I am certain one result would be greater productivity.
8. three
9. Learning how to relax and manage stress can actually improve the productivity of employees.
10. Linked to the need to improve performance and productivity is the need to reduce absenteeism and medical costs.
11. two
12. Stress management has led to lower medical costs and fewer work hours lost due to absenteeism.
13. Stress management programs are very popular because they make good business sense.

14. Our firm can have healthier, happier, more productive employees and higher profits.

15. I hope that your department will consider my suggestion and implement a program to combat stress.

The Short Report

1. National Board of Inquiry said of bombers, "They vanished completely as if they had flown to Mars."

2. pilots, expert flyers, on training mission, Florida, Dec. 5, 1945

3. flight leader to tower: "Can't see land, ocean looks strange, we're completely lost."

4. best known disappearance—five Navy Avenger bombers

5. search produces no life rafts, no plane wrecks, no oil slicks

6. pilots report gyro and magnetic compasses "going crazy"

7. over 100 planes and ships vanished thus far

8. Bermuda Triangle also known as Devil's Triangle

9. no bodies or wreckage from any disappearance ever found

10. points of triangle: Bermuda, southern Florida, Puerto Rico

11. imaginary area off southern Atlantic coast of U.S.

12. more than 1,000 lives lost thus far

13. time-space warp leading to other dimensions

14. UFOs from inner or outer space kidnap vessels

15. electromagnetic force fields

16. Navy supply ship U.S.S. Cyclops with crew of 309 vanished in good weather, March 4, 1918

17. no radio messages, no wreckage of ship found

18. Bermuda Triangle also known as Devil's Triangle

19. imaginary area off southern Atlantic coast of U.S.

20. points of triangle: Bermuda, southern Florida, Puerto Rico

21. over 100 planes and ships vanished thus far

22. more than 1,000 lives lost thus far

23. no bodies or wreckage from any disappearances ever found

24. best known disappearance—five Navy Avenger bombers

25. pilots, expert flyers, on training mission, Florida, Dec. 5, 1945

26. pilots report gyro and magnetic compasses "going crazy"

27. flight leader to tower: "Can't see land, ocean looks strange, we're completely lost."

28. search produces no life rafts, no plane wrecks, no oil slicks

29. National Board of Inquiry said of bombers, "They vanished completely as if they had flown to Mars."

30. Navy supply ship U.S.S. Cyclops with crew of 309 vanished in good weather, March 4, 1918

31. no radio messages, no wreckage of ship found

32. time-space warp leading to other dimensions

33. electromagnetic force fields

34. UFOs from inner or outer space kidnap vessels

The Research Paper

1. Transactional Analysis Defined
2. Three People Inside of You: Parent, Adult, Child
3. Parent Ego State Defined
4. Adult Ego State Defined
5. Child Ego State Defined
6. Know Your Ego State: Your Feelings
7. Know Your Ego State: Your Words
8. Know Your Ego State: Your Actions
9. Know Your Ego State: Others' Reactions
10. Exchange of Strokes: Positive and Negative
11. Hunger for Strokes: Games
12. Applying What You Have Learned

13. 3
14. 4
15. 1
16. 2

17. 5
18. 3
19. 2
20. 4
21. 1
22. 6

23. 3
24. 2
25. 5
26. 1
27. 4

28. 2
29. 3
30. 5
31. 4
32. 1

33. 3
34. 7
35. 6
36. 9
37. 1
38. 2
39. 4
40. 8
41. 5

42. 4
43. 5
44. 1
45. 3
46. 6
47. 2

48. 3
49. 1
50. 4
51. 2

52. 5
53. 4
54. 1
55. 2
56. 3

The Research Paper *(continued)*

57. 4
58. 5
59. 2
60. 1
61. 3

62. 6
63. 5
64. 9
65. 1
66. 2
67. 4
68. 3
69. 8
70. 7

71. 3
72. 4
73. 2
74. 5
75. 1

76. 3
77. 2
78. 4
79. 1